The Virgin Trial

ALSO BY KATE HENNIG

The Last Wife

the
VIRGIN
TRIAL
Kate Hennig

**PLAYWRIGHTS
CANADA PRESS**
Toronto

For professional or amateur production rights, please contact:
The Gary Goddard Agency
149 Church Street, 2nd Floor
Toronto, ON M5B 1Y4
416.928.0299, www.garygoddardagency.com/apply-for-performance-rights/

LIBRARY AND ARCHIVES CANADA CATALOGUING IN PUBLICATION
Hennig, Kate, author
    The virgin trial / Kate Hennig. -- First edition.

Issued in print and electronic formats.
ISBN 978-1-77091-770-5 (softcover).--ISBN 978-1-77091-771-2 (PDF).--
ISBN 978-1-77091-772-9 (HTML).--ISBN 978-1-77091-773-6 (Kindle)

    1. Elizabeth I, Queen of England, 1533-1603--Drama. I. Title.

PS8615.E543V57 2017   C812'.6   C2017-901359-9
                                              C2017-901360-2

We acknowledge the financial support of the Canada Council for the Arts, the Ontario Arts Council (OAC), the Ontario Media Development Corporation, and the Government of Canada through the Canada Book Fund for our publishing activities.

Canada Council   Conseil des arts
for the Arts   du Canada

ONTARIO ARTS COUNCIL
CONSEIL DES ARTS DE L'ONTARIO
an Ontario government agency
un organisme du gouvernement de l'Ontario

Ontario
Ontario Media Development
Corporation

To my dear friend, David Scammell, for thirty-two years of laughter, also for the psychological support you provide to both me and my characters.

This is an *imagining* of history. Oh yes, it is based on actual people and events, and though portions of it are deliciously accurate, some may offend the historically concise among you, while still others are completely and utterly fabricated. My priority in choosing must always favour the dramatic.

What I am deeply interested in is the humanity of these iconic historical characters. I want to imagine what made them do what they did, just as I want to imagine what made Margaret Thatcher, Donald Trump, and Bashar al-Assad do what they did. They are human after all. They have mothers, fathers, siblings, and children. One expects that they play tennis, they watch television, they read books; they laugh, they worry, they drink too much coffee from time to time. It fascinates me to create these personal possibilities and then imagine how they might lead to some of the major decisions that history records. It calls our political self-righteousness into question.

This is a contemporary play. This is a domestic play. No historical costuming or accents required. Diversity in casting is strongly encouraged. This is Bess's story.

—KH

The Virgin Trial was first produced by the Stratford Festival and premiered at the Studio Theatre in Stratford, Ontario, on June 27, 2017, with the following cast and creative team:

Bess: Bahia Watson
Ted: Nigel Bennett
Ashley: Laura Condlin
Mary: Sara Farb
Thom: Brad Hodder
Eleanor: Yanna McIntosh
Parry: André Morin

Artistic director: Antoni Cimolino
Executive director: Anita Gaffney
Producer: David Auster
Casting director: Beth Russell
Creative planning director: Jason Miller

Director: Alan Dilworth
Designer: Yannick Larivée
Lighting designer: Kimberly Purtell
Sound designer: Alexander MacSween
Dramaturge: Bob White
Originating dramaturge: Andy McKim
Fight director: John Stead
Associate fight director: Anita Nittoly
Assistant director: Katrina Darychuk
Stage manager / production stage manager: Meghan Callan
Assistant stage manager: Loreen Gibson

Apprentice stage manager: Christopher Brackett
Production assistant: Troy Taylor
Production stage manager: Meghan Callan
Technical director: Robbin Cheesman
Associate technical director: Eleanor Creelman

This play was commissioned by the Stratford Festival. The playwright gratefully acknowledges the support of the Ontario Arts Council, the Canada Council for the Arts, and the 2015 Banff Playwrights Colony—a partnership between the Banff Centre and the Canada Council for the Arts.

PLAYWRIGHT'S NOTES

From the essay "Virgin Power," first published in the Stratford Festival program for the premiere of *The Virgin Trial*.

"What's a virgin?" my eight-year-old sister asked my father one Christmas in our very brown 1970s family room deep in the suburbs of southwest Calgary. As a sixteen-year-old my eyes bugged right out of my head while waiting with bated breath to hear how he would dig himself out of that one.

"A girl who is not yet married," he replied without a batting of the eye.

Darn. Good answer, I thought, somewhat disappointed at his ease. Of course my father, being a Lutheran minister, was practised in his response to this question, bombarded as he was at this time of year by curious Christmas-pageant performers.

Elizabeth I would also be pleased with his answer. The fact that it makes no mention of sexual intercourse would support the cult of innocence that was constructed around her: she was Gloriana, the Virgin Queen.

But though my father's answer was enough to satisfy my younger sister, it was certainly not the whole truth. It was a convenient truth.

I would venture to say that the professed virginity of the second queen regnant of England is also a convenient truth. It has extensive dramatic possibilities—and we know how this princess loved dramatic possibilities. Might we even consider her a *creative artist*?

What if Elizabeth *created* a campaign of virginity to distract the masses from her dubious integrity?

What if this *girl who is not-yet married* was in full control of her destiny even in her teenage years?

Out of necessity, she imagined her own pristine narrative in the face of a life-threatening scandal; a wily teenager, well-trained in the arts of deception, she then put a spin on the facts to whitewash her part in a variety of extremely suspicious circumstances; this young Elizabeth was capable at a very young age of making choices that would determine her highly potent future.

But she was only a *girl*. Can a *girl* really be capable of such foresight?

Ha! We don't give girls enough credit.

In 1549, Elizabeth was doing exactly what girls and young women are doing today: adapting, reinventing her own image, pursuing her *self* as art, utilizing her unique principles and prescient solutions to achieve her goals.

Call it girl power. Call it virgin power. Both then, and now, it's the beating heart of my play.

A forward slash (/) indicates the next speaker should overlap their dialogue at the slash; when this occurs at the beginning of a line, the next speaker completely overlaps that line.

An em dash (—) at the end of a line indicates that the thought should be cut off, either by the current speaker or by the next speaker jumping in.

An ellipsis (. . .) indicates that the speaker should search briefly for the thought, leaving a gap in speech.

In the premiere production of this play, under the direction of Alan Dilworth, the interview setting stayed present and Bess stayed on stage as the scenes from the past invaded her memory. It was an excellent way to solve the back-and-forthing.

I know that most [people]—not only those considered clever, but even those who are very clever, and capable of understanding most difficult scientific, mathematical, or philosophic problems—can very seldom discern even the simplest and most obvious truth if it be such as to oblige them to admit the falsity of conclusions they have formed, perhaps with much difficulty—conclusions of which they are proud, which they have taught others, and in which they have built their lives.

—Leo Tolstoy, "What is Art?"

CHARACTERS

Bess: a princess; thirteen to fifteen years old; *intelligent, precocious, entitled, unedited, sexual; fire*

Mary: a princess; thirty to thirty-two years old; *private, cutting, wounded, capable, loyal; water*

Eleanor: a lady of the court; fiftyish; *contained, obsessive, incisive, independent, vengeful; earth*

Ashley: a lady of the court, governess to Bess; fortyish; *guileless, reliable, effortless, unrefined, maternal; water*

Thom: Lord High Admiral, husband to Katherine Parr; thirty-nine to forty-one years old; *athletic, reckless, impulsive, ineffectual, loving; air*

Ted: Lord Protector to Edward VI, brother to Thom; fifty-ish; *paternal, jovial, authoritative, patient, devoted; earth*

Parry: A lord of the court, secretary to Bess; thirty-fiveish; *buoyant, cheerful, sensitive, abrupt, nervous; air*

ACT ONE
INTERVIEW ONE—JANUARY 19, 1549

> *At table.* BESS *is seated, wearing a dress that has one frill too many. Waiting. After some time* ELEANOR *enters carrying a tray with a pitcher of water and tumblers, a stack of five files, a notepad and pen. She sets down the tray; places the water and tumblers on the table; places the files, notepad, and pen at the end of the table opposite* BESS.

ELEANOR   Water?

> BESS *looks at* ELEANOR. *Looks away.*

Hello?

Did you want a glass of water.

BESS   Are you addressing me?

ELEANOR   It's a small room.

I was told to ask.

BESS   Oh. Sorry. I'll have tea. If I may.

ELEANOR   No tea.

BESS   No tea? Oh. No thank you then.

ELEANOR	Suit yourself.
BESS	But very kind of you to ask.

ELEANOR takes a seat by the notepad and pen. She waits.

ELEANOR	He'll be here soon.
BESS	Ted?
ELEANOR	The Lord Protector.
BESS	Right.

A moment.

ELEANOR	I'm the woman in the room: no "he said she said."
BESS	No what?
ELEANOR	False accusations.
BESS	Am I here to accuse someone of something?
ELEANOR	Never mind. He'll deal with you when he gets here.
BESS	Have I said something to offend you? It was inadvertent if I have. Sometimes people are intimidated by me and I / think
ELEANOR	I know what you've done. I know what your mother did, so don't try to be coy with me. You . . . are a treasonous little bastard.

TED enters with a file of papers. ELEANOR picks up her pen.
TED throws his file onto the table and charges toward BESS.

TED	Elizabeth Tudor, look at you!!

TED throws his arms around BESS.

BESS	Good morning, Ted.
TED	You— Look, Eleanor: such a young lady! Last time I saw you, you were— *(blanking)* Huh! when was the last time I saw you?

BESS	Father's funeral.
TED	Two years?! No, it can't be.
BESS	Almost exactly.
TED	We should see each other more often! I hate it when work gets in the way of family, right, Eleanor? Can't wait to retire. You watch. I'll be a nuisance to you then! You'll be like: "Uncle Ted, coming for lunch again!!" Ha, ha, ha! Don't you think, Eleanor?

TED picks up the file of papers and lays it at the end of the table close to ELEANOR.

(to BESS) How was your trip?

BESS	I don't much like travelling in January; do you?

ELEANOR begins to write at the top of her notepad. TED places his hand on her pen, still looking at BESS.

TED	*(to ELEANOR)* Aw, come on, not yet.
ELEANOR	/ I
TED	We don't have to go on the record yet, do we? Give us a chance to catch up a bit.

TED pours some water in a tumbler and places it near BESS.

Yup. The roads in January. It's like people have never seen snow. And the winters just seem to get worse instead of better, don't they? When I was a kid— Oh, ho, here I go: "When I was a kid . . . "! Blah, blah, blah!

BESS	Anyway . . . It's a cold day to go out.
TED	True. True. But then you had to know you'd be summoned.
BESS	Summoned? Is that what this is?
TED	Did nobody tell you? *(scolding)* Eleanor.

(to BESS) Yuh, yuh, sorry to say: it's, uh, serious business.

BESS	It must be very serious business to arrest the sister of a king.
TED	Oh, you're not under arrest.
BESS	Am I not?
TED	No, no, that'd be way overstepping the mark. You're just . . . here to answer a few questions.
BESS	Well. That's fine then. So long as I'm free to go.
TED	Free to go, free to come over for dinner tonight if you like!
BESS	Dinner? I did ask for tea, but / if
TED	*(to ELEANOR)* No tea?
ELEANOR	No tea.
TED	Right. Well. Eleanor's got the keys to the cupboard, if you know what I mean.

TED takes his cue from the implacable ELEANOR.

Now then. We've got to get down to business: I hope that's okay?

BESS	Yup. That's okay.
TED	So, so, so: you do know that Thom's been arrested.
BESS	I heard.
TED	Good. And I must remind you—but, only as a matter of protocol—

He motions to ELEANOR, who picks up her pen and begins to take notes.

that you hold no rank in this room, understand? You're just a subject of King Edward: same as me, same as Eleanor here. Does that make sense to you?

BESS	That sounds fine.

TED   Nothing to worry about. No, no, no. I'm the protector: here to protect you, just as much as I'm here to protect Eddie. This is all just standard stuff that has to be gone through when someone you're—well . . . *associated* with I guess is the best way of putting it—is arrested.

BESS   I will certainly tell you all I know.

TED   *(to ELEANOR)* She is such a good sport, is our Bess.

> *TED opens the file, picks up the top document, and reads:*

Right.

"The Lord High Admiral, Thomas Seymour, has been arrested and charged with high treason. It is suspected that with the help of several associates both inside and outside the court, he attempted to assault the person of King Edward, most likely for the purpose of kidnapping, but quite possibly with intent to murder."

BESS   Oh.

TED   I know.

"An alarm was raised by the barking of the young king's spaniel, which the perpetrator proceeded to shoot dead."

BESS   Oooh no / oo

TED   "When the room was entered, and light established, the only thing found was the lifeless corpse of the dog."

> *TED pours a tumbler of water for himself and takes a sip.*

Never shoot the dog. How can things possibly go well for anyone who shoots a dog?

BESS   Is Eddie okay?

TED   You see, Eleanor: worried about her brother.

(to BESS) Eddie's totally fine. Thank God.

ELEANOR looks up from her notepad at BESS. BESS is enthralled. TED returns to his document:

"We have reason to suspect that this unlawful entry and assault on King Edward was the culmination of an ongoing plot of Seymour's to overthrow the current leadership, to marry the princess Elizabeth—"

BESS inadvertently swallows.

"second daughter of the late King Henry the Eighth, and establish himself as her consort should she succeed to the throne. It must be noted that the princess Elizabeth is also under *grave suspicion*."

BESS   Me?

ELEANOR   You.

> *TED puts the document in front of BESS. TED sits on the edge of the table.*

TED   Don't worry, don't worry. You're innocent.

BESS   I'm—? Is that what I say? I'm innocent?

TED   *(with a chuckle)* Of course that's what you say! This whole thing was Thom's fault. He's put us all in danger.

BESS   Are you in danger?

TED   My reputation certainly is. The family name. People have this obsession with genetic predisposition, know what I mean?

BESS   I do.

TED   But I'm not so much worried about me. People trust me. It's *you*: people don't really know you, and . . .

BESS   What . . . ?

TED   Well, all this "gun in the palace" business, it's disquieted the masses—there's scandal in the air.

BESS	*(sensing the intrigue)* Scandal. Ahah. The vultures will gather.
TED	*(a good analogy)* Oh, you are so right. The vultures have a whiff in their noses. A whiff of Thomas . . . and *you*.
	They smell a faction building. Which only leads to an opposing faction building, and pretty soon? Civil war. Nobody wants that, do they?
BESS	No way.
TED	It was only your grandfather that put an end to the last one—
BESS	With the Roses.
TED	Two princes dead in the tower. That's what comes of family fighting each other for a throne. And our foreign enemies, well they look at the three of you siblings and—
BESS	Half siblings.
TED	—exactly—and see the writing on the wall.
BESS	Heightened-alert levels. International intrigue.
TED	*(another chuckle)* You've even got the lingo!
BESS	D'you think *my* reputation is at stake?
TED	Your future! your marriageability, certainly your political profile. If you're implicated in this mess, I mean, how can the people of England love you as *their* princess? Trust you to wait your turn?
	No, no, no. Just tell me—tell us—all you know about this plot—
BESS	Plot?
TED	—simple as that. We just have to make it official, you see? That's why we're here. We're gonna take this *(the document)* "grave suspicion" and clear up the stink.

TED puts the document on the table in front of BESS. BESS picks up a pencil and stabs the document.

BESS   Ha, ha—take that, you vultures!

ELEANOR   This is not for your entertainment.

TED   Oh, now, Eleanor, for heaven's sake, let her enjoy herself. She's never been in a situation like this, have you, Bess?

BESS   Never.

TED   *(to ELEANOR)* See.

(to BESS, casually) Oh. Almost forgot: if any of your answers reveal evidence, or . . . if testimony surfaces that allies you to this sedition, we'll have no choice but to arrest you for treason.

This lands on BESS.

BESS   Treason? You never said / that

TED   Sure, you know all about treason, don't you. That "genetic predisposition," right? Though me? I'm not interested in drawing any similarities between you and your mother. The only thing I really need to know about / is

ELEANOR   Is your relationship with Thomas Seymour.

BESS doesn't move.

AN APT VESSEL—FEBRUARY 1547

At table. BESS is studying. THOM enters with a book.

THOM   Hi, Bess.

BESS   Hi, Thom.

THOM   I— Am I intruding . . . ?

BESS   I'm—

       BESS indicates her books.

       School work.

THOM   Feeling better?

BESS   Day by day.

THOM   The funeral was hard. He was a big man, your father.

       BESS makes an awkward smile.

       Right. Ha. In more ways than one.

BESS   You're not going back to Amsterdam?

THOM   A permanent member of Council now.

BESS   A desktop admiral.

THOM   I . . . command the ships in my office.

       A little gap of nothing.

BESS   Have you come to help me with my paper?

THOM   Kate said—the, uh, *queen* said you— But if this isn't a good time—

BESS   It's about ships.

THOM   Yeah.

BESS   I like ships.

THOM   Me too.

       BESS holds up the book she's been reading.

       Naval Leaders in the Battle of Artemisium. Ahah: the Greeks and the Persians.

BESS   I'm trying to compare it with something current. In an essay. Kate said—the, uh, *queen*—said you could talk to me about, about when you were commander in the Battle of the Solent.

THOM   You want to write about your dad's ship.

BESS   The *Mary Rose*.

THOM   Oh, she was yare.

BESS   What does that mean: "she was yare."

THOM   She was ready.

BESS   Ready for what?

THOM   To take the sea: a fine, fast, sturdy vessel, with . . . magnificently huge buttocks.

BESS   *(exploding with laughter)* Buttocks?!

THOM   Oh shoot. That's not a naval term, is it.

BESS   I don't think so!!

THOM   *(joining her laughter)* She was, you know, like—

> *He demonstrates the wide, round hull of the boat, at the same time jokingly taking in* BESS's *bum.*

BESS   *(scandalized)* Tho-om! You are so—

Show me. Show me how the battle started. I have it here . . .

> BESS *opens a map. And they begin to create the scene.*

THOM   Right, so, Portsmouth Harbour . . .

BESS   All closed in. The land comes right around.

THOM   Tight as a gnat's chuff.

BESS   *(laughing at the dirty joke)* Oh my / gosh

THOM   Unprepared we / were.

BESS   What's a / chuff?

THOM   And suddenly the French were on us. Over two hundred ships to our eighty.

BESS   So what do you do then?

THOM   Stay calm. Assess the opposition: what do they want? How will they try to get it?

BESS   And so you . . . ?

THOM   Created a flank, and shot broadside.

BESS   Uhuh.

THOM   Never go on the offensive when you're outmanned and out-gunned. First rule of naval warfare.

BESS   *(writing)* "Never go on the offensive when you're—" But then why did she sink?

THOM   Never found out:

> THOM *draws* BESS *back to the map.*

we were tacking to intercept their landing parties!

BESS   *(looks at the map, the penny drops)* Oh! Like a gnat's chuff!

THOM   Sometimes you have to abandon the sinking ship in order to stop the invasion.

BESS   *(writing)* "Sometimes you have to abandon"— So Father's best ship ends up at the bottom of the Solent.

> BESS *looks at* THOM, *who is quite close to her. He looks at her, then away.*

THOM   Now then, comparing that battle with the Persians and the / Greeks

BESS   I need a commander.

THOM   Oh. I don't remember / his name

BESS   Not for my essay.

THOM	For—?
BESS	For me. If . . . if I was to need a commander, for a fleet, or for an army . . . would you? do that? for me?

THOM laughs.

THOM	Are you going to war, Bess?

BESS laughs.

BESS	In my mind.

A moment between them.

We need to establish naval superiority.

THOM	We . . . ?
BESS	England. Our fleet.
THOM	Uhuh.
BESS	Eddie—well, *Ted*—
THOM	Bloody Ted—
BESS	The Lord Protector wants to wipe out the Spanish pirates in the Channel. But we need to negotiate allegiances with them to maximize our trading potential.
THOM	Do . . . we.
BESS	We . . . do.
THOM	Anything else we need besides . . . a willingness to negotiate?
BESS	Courage. To bend the rules.
THOM	Rules save lives.
BESS	Break the rules. There are no rules.
THOM	I've never been very—
BESS	Scatter the pieces and watch them roll under the couch.

A moment between them. THOM *hands* BESS *the book he brought.*

THOM This is for you. For your essay.

BESS *The Mary Rose: Tudor's Naval Glory.*

THOM There's something else in there for you.

BESS For me?

> BESS *opens the book and finds a letter. She begins to open it.*

THOM Later.

> THOM *puts his hand on* BESS'*s.*

When you're alone, okay?

BESS Okay.

> *As he goes:*

THOM Oh, Bess . . .

BESS Yes, Thom?

THOM *(not giving anything away)* When you're Queen . . . I'll be your commander.

INTERVIEW TWO—JANUARY 19, 1549

> *At table.* BESS *and* ELEANOR *are seated as before.* TED *walks a perimeter.*

TED No wonder you felt a bit at sea.

BESS At sea?

TED In the wake of it all. So many people reaching for position. I can't imagine how you dealt with it.

BESS He'd been sick a long time.

TED   But to lose such a— Your father was a big man.

BESS smiles.

BESS   Lucky for Eddie then.

TED   In what way lucky?

BESS   That in all that chaos you managed to kick Kate out and
        become Protector yourself.

For the first time TED considers BESS in a different light.

TED   You think the country could run better with someone else
        in charge?

BESS   Isn't my brother in charge?

And then it's gone.

TED   *(to ELEANOR)* You see that! Would you look at how clever
        she is!

        (to BESS) Good one, Bess! You bet Eddie's in charge.

ELEANOR   Are you questioning the protector's authority?

BESS   No. I'm merely clarifying his qualifications for that title.

TED   Ahah! You're concerned with the way titles are accrued,
        are you?

BESS   Me? I have no need to be.

TED   Well, *we're* interested in titles, aren't we, Eleanor.

ELEANOR   Mmhmm.

TED   And it's the admiral's, well, *determined quest* for a *ranking
        title* that we're most interested in.

        After your dad died did you, uh, receive a letter from
        Thomas Seymour?

BESS   Absolutely.

TED   You did.

BESS	I got hundreds of letters. I mean, people were so genuinely sad, but—Thom's letter was different.
TED	Very different, I'd say.
BESS	He seemed to understand the shock that happens when someone you love is—

BESS inadvertently triggers a recent memory. Her eyes suddenly fill with tears.

	Sorry. I'd rather not talk about it.
TED	Aw, sweetie, do you need to take a little break?
ELEANOR	/ No!
BESS	No. It just feels so fresh.
ELEANOR	Moving on then . . .
TED	Right. Yes. No. This letter from Thom wasn't a condolence. It was kind of a weird letter to be honest, but we think it showed the admiral's interest in achieving another title, don't we, Eleanor.
	This letter . . . was a proposal of marriage.
BESS	Marriage.
TED	Marriage to the person second in line to the English throne.
BESS	That's me.
ELEANOR	We know.
TED	It was a strange series of events, I'll say that:
	Thom came to Council, only days after your dad passed away, with a request to marry you or marry Mary—"marry Mary"! Ha, ha, ha.
	The Council put the kibosh on it, naturally. But Thom ignored our objection and sent letters anyway: one to you, one to your sister. Good thing neither of you bit.

So then he settled for Kate.

BESS   *(tautly)* He didn't *settle* for Kate. Kate and Thom were very much in love. We all know that.

TED   Which only makes his letters more perplexing. So, I wondered what your response was.

BESS   To the queen's marriage?

TED   *(to ELEANOR)* Ha! Clever. You see!

   (to BESS) No, no, no. To Thom's proposal.

SAY YES TO THE DRESS—JUNE 1547

In private. ASHLEY is making a shopping list; BESS is looking at a portfolio of fabric swatches; PARRY is making entries in a ledger while at the same time demonstrating his knowledge of fashion.

PARRY   White dupioni silk. It's like shantung, but the slub gives it more texture. And lightly shot with gold, I think. Don't you think?

BESS   Cloth of gold brocade is my favourite.

PARRY   For the kirtle, yes: good idea.

ASHLEY   Kirtle?

PARRY   *(of ASHLEY)* Pleb.

BESS   *(clarifying)* The underskirt.

PARRY   *(to BESS)* Thank you. Once we set a date I'll draw up a separate budget line for the dress. I have connections in Italy who'll custom weave something for us, and then John Malte can make some serious magic with his sheers.

BESS   *(He's a superstar.)* John Malte!

ASHLEY   Who's John Malte?

> *PARRY and BESS exchange a look. Then back to ASHLEY:*

PARRY
& BESS   Pleb.

PARRY   I'll need to shift funds from the catering budget. How do we feel about going vegetarian for a year?

BESS   Can I have *red* shoes for my wedding?

ASHLEY   A year?

PARRY   Shoes! Good Lord.

ASHLEY   Really?

PARRY   A sensible heel, I think—

ASHLEY   / Hmmm.

PARRY   —we don't want you to look like one of those fools who can't manage their stilettos on cobblestones.

ASHLEY   No meat.

BESS   Gold shoes, maybe? To go with the silk?

PARRY   Gold. *(adjusting ledger entry)* Maybe two years.

ASHLEY   Not even fish?

BESS   And those little triangle points on sleeves that come down onto your hand? I want those.

PARRY   Messy and Thommie sitting in a tree

PARRY &
ASHLEY   / K-I-S-S

> *BESS swats PARRY playfully.*

BESS   / Shut uuup! Not fair!

> *PARRY runs and BESS chases.*

PARRY &	
ASHLEY	I-N-G. First comes love, then comes

THOM enters. The game ends rather self-consciously.

THOM	Hi. Sorry. There was no— I, uh, let myself in.
BESS	Hi, Thom!
THOM	Hi, Bess. Ashley. Parry.
ASHLEY	/ Hello.
PARRY	Lord Admiral.
THOM	Oh please, not the title. I'm still Thom, right? Still Thom.
PARRY	Sure: Thom. Soon to / be
BESS	Parry!
PARRY	So, were you just . . . in the neighbourhood?
THOM	No. I came—

Here. I brought chocolates. Belgian chocolates.

PARRY	Mmmm. Chocolates.
THOM	From Belgium. Pralines, actually.
BESS	Thanks.
THOM	I know you like them.

BESS smiles. THOM touches her hand as she accepts the gift.

I, uh—needed to share something with you, and . . . well, I think it's good news.

THOM tries to think of a way to get BESS alone.

I wondered if maybe . . .

He decides that perhaps the direct and public approach will save them both some discomfort.

The queen and I have been married. Privately.

I mean, we got married, Kate and I. Kate and me.
I—

There is a silence, and then PARRY *laughs.*

PARRY   Oh my God, hysterical!

Right?

THOM remains serious.

THOM   We, uh . . . we cleared it with Eddie, and for sure we were gonna get married before, but then your dad came along and . . . suddenly she was wife number six, so. Kate's really happy, I . . . I know you want her to be happy; she's been such a good mother to you, and . . .

Yeah. So . . .

BESS puts the chocolates on the table.

ASHLEY   Congratulations. I mean, that's certainly a step up for you. Marrying a queen.

THOM   Dowager Queen.

ASHLEY   I think . . . you'll make a terrific couple. Bess?

PARRY   And we do want Kate to be happy. Don't we. We do. Don't we? Really.

ASHLEY   Bess?

BESS   *(still looking at* THOM*)* Yes?

(to ASHLEY*)* Of course. Happy.

THOM now looks at BESS, and she at him. Both are confused.

THOM   I—we—Kate wants you to stay living with her—with us—here at Chelsea. We, we both think it will be best for you—for us—to be a family.

ASHLEY   Best . . . for—?

PARRY	And here we thought we might be moving to *your* neck of the woods.
THOM	I hope . . . I hope you'll stay. I know that's what Kate wants. And she has no reason to think that you would want anything else . . . if you . . . know what I mean.
BESS	It only makes sense that I stay. When *you* move in with *us*.
THOM	Oh, and there was that letter I gave you, several months ago now, and—you've probably forgotten it, ha—but I thought maybe you could dispose of that letter, probably best, and that it might be kept a secret just between us and— Does that make sense?
BESS	It all seems perfectly . . .
PARRY	Timed.
ASHLEY	I'm sure we'll get over any expectation we / may have
THOM	Good! Then. I'll, uh, let myself out the way I came in.
BESS	Thank you for the pralines.
THOM	Sorry?
BESS	The chocolates.
THOM	Plenty more where those came from. Ha.

THOM goes. BESS watches him go. BESS crumples.

ASHLEY	Oh my Messy Bessy.
PARRY	Straight men: un-fucking-believable.

> *At table.* BESS *sits at one end of the table,* ELEANOR *at the other.* ELEANOR *looks across the table at* BESS.

ELEANOR You're like your mother in more ways than one.

BESS Which mother?

ELEANOR She also came across as dumb.

BESS Sticks and stones may break my / bones

ELEANOR You're not even sentimental.

BESS Should I be?

ELEANOR For mothers? People expect it.

BESS I have no memory of Anne Boleyn. She died before I was three.

ELEANOR I have plenty of memories of Anne Boleyn. 'D you like a few of mine?

> ELEANOR *rises. She picks up the five files.*

(placing each file in front of BESS*)* Henry Norris, Frank Weston, Bill Brereton . . .

BESS Should I know / these

ELEANOR Mark Smeaton: the musician, and . . . the second Viscount Rochford: her brother George.

Five counts of adultery. Have a look.

> BESS *timidly opens the top file.*

BESS Where's Ted?

> ELEANOR *points to the document in front of* BESS.

ELEANOR An eyewitness account of your mom and her brother: read it.

BESS	I / don't
ELEANOR	*(not raising her voice)* Read it.
BESS	"Her tongue in his mouth, and his in hers."
ELEANOR	Incest.

BESS is shocked and frightened. She turns the article over.

Shame, shame.

ELEANOR holds the article up in front of BESS's face.

Once a woman's sexual exploits are exposed . . . there's simply no taking that picture out of your head. Let alone out of the public consciousness.

BESS	Is that right.
ELEANOR	"The Great Whore": that's how people remember your mother. And deviance begets deviance. Your little trysts with Thom are just the beginning.
BESS	Thom: that's who we're here to talk about. Not my mother. Not me.

Where's Ted?

ELEANOR	It's not merely promiscuity you share: your mother had no empathy either.
BESS	I'm not sure I understand what empathy is.
ELEANOR	Mhmm. And I'm trying to expose that little flaw to the uninformed public.
BESS	The public know me. They see me for who I am.
ELEANOR	The public sees you for forty-five seconds as you pass by in an open carriage on parade from one of your great houses to another. They have no idea who you are. They paint a portrait that gives them comfort, that's all. They can just as easily black out the entire canvas and start again.

BESS	White.
ELEANOR	Sorry?
BESS	They can just as easily *white* out the entire canvas and start again.

A moment.

ELEANOR	You know I can't kill you. Can't . . . *press* you to determine your involvement. But I can certainly slap you into prison, pretty picture and all.
BESS	Eddie won't allow that.
ELEANOR	Won't he.
BESS	Eddie loves me.
ELEANOR	Is that what you think.
BESS	Besides, there's Mary! She comes next after Eddie, not me.
ELEANOR	Oh, I haven't forgotten about Mary; I just haven't figured out your plan to get rid of her.
BESS	/ Get rid—?
ELEANOR	You must know the English people will never follow anyone who killed her virtuous sister.
BESS	Kill Mary?
ELEANOR	*You* may not be sentimental, but *they* most certainly are. Poison, maybe? Is that it? She hasn't been in the peak of health, completely out of the picture since Eddie's been king; people'll think she succumbed to her illness. I'd say poison's a good idea.

> Isn't that what Thom did to Katherine Parr in order to get to you?

BESS	SHUT UP! SHUT. UP.

ELEANOR attacks this crack in the veneer.

ELEANOR	Whoo—touched a / nerve?
BESS	Don't you dare suggest / that—
ELEANOR	That Thom might have it in him to kill another human being?
	Or that you might?
BESS	*(petulant)* I want to see Ted!
ELEANOR	He'll be back soon. He's busy with another prisoner.

This word lands on BESS.

BESS	Another—? I'm not a prisoner.

ELEANOR looks at BESS and lets her sit with her own statement.

I'm not a prisoner. *Thom* is a prisoner.

INTERVENTION—JANUARY 19, 1549

In private. THOM is alone in a prison cell, miserably hung-over. TED enters and stands in the doorway.

THOM	*(under his breath)* Ahhh fuck. *(louder)* I don't want to see you.

TED doesn't budge.

(slightly too loud) I don't want to see you! Can't you hear! I don't want to see anyone.

(conversational) Can I have some water?

TED	Of course.
THOM	Of course?
TED	Sheets, pillowcases, even soap and a towel: you're my brother.

THOM	If I wasn't your brother?
TED	*(a joke)* No catered lunch.

A moment.

THOM	What do you want?
TED	To help. Only to help. Promise.
THOM	Get out. I told the chamberlain. Why does nobody listen to what I want?
TED	No really, Thommie: the family's worried.
THOM	Worried are they—the great Seymour family—for their respectability?
TED	For you. For you.
THOM	Yeah well, I can take care of myself. It's my life, right? You don't get a say. Dad doesn't get a say. Eleanor for sure doesn't get a say. Me. I get a say. That's it.

(his terrible headache) Can I get something for my head? With the water?

TED	Of course.
THOM	Of course.
TED	We were just— We'd hoped it wouldn't get this far. We'd hoped you'd reach a point where you could see that your . . . obsession, / your
THOM	My addiction. My goddamn addiction . . .
TED	Exactly. And we're trying to help / you
THOM	Oh, and I've let you down. This time. That time. The time before.

What? What can I do about that *now*?

Go ahead. Say you told me so. Say / it!

TED	No, no, no: I'm not here about the past.
THOM	Then what do you want?
TED	We— We're hoping the lack of access to her will allow you / to
THOM	To what. To see the light?
TED	It's *her*! You can tell me. I know it's her. She's responsible / for all
THOM	Shut up. SHUT. UP. *I'm here. I* shot the fucking dog, not her. Deal with *me*!
TED	Absolutely.

A moment.

So.

I'll have them bring water. Towels. Anything else? Oh, and something for your head.

TED starts to go.

THOM	My head.

TED stops.

Will they . . . chop it off?

A moment.

TED	*(from the heart)* I'll do everything in my power to see that doesn't happen.
THOM	*(beside himself with regret)* Christ. What have I done? You don't know what I've done!
TED	Just *tell* me then, and I can talk / to the—
THOM	*(a way out)* What if I kill myself. That would be the *noble* thing to do. I'll take care of it and spare them the expense.
TED	Don't say that. Now I have to—

TED looks at THOM and makes a decision.

Give me your belt. And your shoes.

THOM   Don't be ridi / culous

TED   I have no choice. You have to give them to me.

THOM takes off his belt and his shoes and hands them to TED.

THOM   I'm / not going to

TED   I'll have the chamberlain look in on you.

THOM   You should hate me. You have every right to hate me. I hate you.

TED   I'll come every day. Twice a day.

TED heads for the door.

THOM   Say hi to her for me.

TED makes a little half-smile of resignation and goes. THOM holds his head and considers his fate.

INTERVIEW THREE, PART TWO— JANUARY 19, 1549

At table. BESS and ELEANOR continue.

ELEANOR   Doesn't have the strongest moral compass, does he.

Thom is not innocent.

But then neither was Kate. In fact, the primary female influences in your life were both women of questionable / virtue—

BESS   Stop talking.

ELEANOR —and what Katherine Parr allowed to happen to you, under her own roof, bordered on child / abuse.

TED enters.

TED Oh. Did I interrupt something?

BESS Where have you been? You can't leave me alone with her.

TED Why?

(to ELEANOR) Are you being naughty? I'll have to send you over to Ashley and Parry if you don't behave in front of the princess.

BESS A-Ashley and Parry? They're here?

TED Down the hall.

BESS They— They shouldn't be here.

ELEANOR Potential witnesses.

BESS They have nothing to do with this.

ELEANOR We'll determine that.

TED We know Thom didn't act alone.

Oh. I saw Thom, too. You want to know how he's doing?

BESS says nothing.

Sobered up.

Considering his options.

A beat.

He says hi.

TED walks a perimeter. He looks over ELEANOR's shoulder at her notes.

BESS Eleanor wants me to slander Thom and Kate.

TED	I don't care about Thom and *Kate*; I want to understand the relationship between Thom and *you*. Can you clarify that for me?
BESS	He was my mother's husband.
TED	Y-yes, but there were rumours circulating at the / time
BESS	Of course. Yes. They were everywhere.
TED	. . . when you were living with Kate and Thom at Chelsea.
BESS	Reports that Thom was seen in my room.
TED	Uhuh. And what was he doing in your room?
BESS	He came to wake me. *They* came. Together.
TED	He was seen alone. In his nightshirt.

BESS takes a sip of her water.

BESS	Can I please have a cup of tea?
TED	Look, I get it: my kid brother's a good-looking guy. Women go silly over him; they always have. Even Eleanor thinks he's cute. It would be perfectly normal if you were . . . feeling . . . some . . . feelings for him.
BESS	Why don't we all have a cup of tea?
TED	Did you lead him on, maybe?
BESS	. . . make a whole pot.
TED	Why did Kate send you away?
BESS	I wasn't sent away as a punishment, if that's what you're thinking. Ha, ha! No. Kate was my protector. She knew how things worked. She knew people in this court would try to drag down someone like me—someone above them— because that would make them feel strong. Important. That's how it is when you have no real power of your own: you try to take it from others. Kate sent me away from Chelsea to

protect me from exactly that. From being dragged through the mud by people like . . . *(TED and ELEANOR)* that.

> *BESS takes a moment to consider her strategy.*

You want details, right?

TED   Details are good.

BESS   Fine. To start with: Thom did come to my room.

> *A moment.*

Should I say more?

TED   Please.

BESS   On several occasions.

> *A moment.*

TED   Anything else?

BESS   *(a fact)* Um . . . We . . . played tickle . . .

TED   Tickle: and . . . ?

BESS   I don't remember a nightshirt.

ELEANOR   *(calling BESS's bluff)* But you can't possibly forget what happened in the Chelsea garden with Thom and Kate and that black wool dress.

> *BESS is caught off guard. She blanches. ELEANOR notices this.*

BESS   I . . . I mean there's got to be tea somewhere in this tower.

TED   *(looking for details)* Thom had keys made for your room.

BESS   He had keys made for all the doors in the house he lived in.

ELEANOR   *(methodically on the subject of the garden)* You think what happened in the garden qualifies as part of their pristine relationship?

> *BESS ignores ELEANOR. ELEANOR takes a note.*

TED	He chased you and the other household girls through your chambers.
BESS	We played hide and seek. Sometimes Mother May I.
TED	That's all?
BESS	Of course. I love playing games.

HIDE AND SEEK—AUGUST 1547

In public. BESS *is hiding.* PARRY *walks through with some ledgers. Simultaneously, from off, we hear:*

ASHLEY	Ready or not, here I come!!
PARRY	Oh, you kids.
BESS	Shhhhh, Parry. I'm hiding . . .
PARRY	Okay, okay.

BESS hides under the table. PARRY *opens his books on top of the table.* THOM *runs in.*

BESS	*(an excited whisper)* Thom!
THOM	Shhhh.
BESS	She's coming. *She's coming!*

THOM hides with BESS. *There is a moment of anticipation. In on the game,* PARRY *pretends to organize his ledgers at the table.*

THOM	So you *do* understand?
BESS	Sure.
THOM	That day with the pralines—

BESS	No excuses needed: it's months ago now; I've forgotten all about it.
THOM	It's not an / excuse
BESS	Promises can't always be kept, right, Parry?
PARRY	Not always.
BESS	You're not the first person to break a promise. You won't be the last.
THOM	I-I didn't promise. It / was
BESS	Let me finish.
	I know what you wanted back then, but . . .
PARRY	Events played out another way.
THOM	I never meant to mislead you.
BESS	There are worse things you could do, right? And I'd still be your friend.
THOM	You would. I think you would.
BESS	I'm not won with trifles. Nor lost with them.
THOM	Trifles . . . ? I-I—

There is a moment between them. Then ASHLEY runs in.

ASHLEY	*(to PARRY)* Have you seen them?

THOM slaps BESS soundly on the bum.

BESS	Ow!!
THOM	*(to BESS)* Run!!

BESS runs out.

BESS	*(as she goes)* Whoever kisses Kate last is a rotten egg!

THOM is about to follow but ASHLEY puts herself between him and the door.

THOM	She bumped into me!
PARRY	She's just getting over / your last
THOM	That's what—you heard us—that's what we were talking about.
ASHLEY	Don't start toying around / with
THOM	I'm not! I'm playing hide and seek.

THOM hesitates.

ASHLEY	Well, hurry up then.
PARRY	You'll be a rotten egg!

THOM runs out. ASHLEY and PARRY exchange a look.

He has his eye on her again.

ASHLEY	*(disgusted)* He's barely been married three months!

ASHLEY goes.

PARRY	*(after her)* Bess was blushing.

PARRY goes back to the table and packs up his ledgers.

(to himself) Just telling you what I saw.

He's so darn handsome.

What's a girl to do?

HIDDEN MOTIVE ONE—JANUARY 20, 1549

In private. ASHLEY sits on a wooden box. ELEANOR holds a cotton sack in her hands.

ELEANOR	It's curious how their relationship developed. While they were both at Chelsea.
ASHLEY	How could it not. They were living under the same roof.

ELEANOR	To the point where she went out on the barge with him unchaperoned.
ASHLEY	Family. No need for a chaperone.
ELEANOR	Different than other girls her age? More mature?
ASHLEY	She loves her independence. I wasn't going to treat her like a baby.
ELEANOR	Fourteen. A girl. Not a woman.
ASHLEY	Kinda hard to say at that age. She knew her limits.
ELEANOR	And you allowed her to determine those limits?
ASHLEY	Look, I have years of experience with her. Which you don't have. You think it would help to forbid her?
ELEANOR	I think she was *fourteen*! Thirteen when he moved in with them. She needed a firm hand. To corral her behaviour. Unless *she* was dictating the boundaries even then.
ASHLEY	What do you think she was doing on that boat?
ELEANOR	Alone. At night. With a man. On the Thames. Let's see . . .
ASHLEY	Yeah, yeah: you're all conjecture and judgment about what a forty-year-old man and a fourteen-year-old girl get up to alone at night.
ELEANOR	Will you listen to what you just said?!
ASHLEY	The barge—Bess was on the barge with Kate's permission— at her bidding even—for a school project.
ELEANOR	Ahah. And did *Bess* choose the Lord High Admiral as instructor?
ASHLEY	A pretty elite teacher, wouldn't you say?

In public. BESS *and* THOM *are on the deck of a barge on the Thames.* BESS *holds a small telescope and is looking up into the night sky.*

THOM   The Winter Circle: it's like a constellation.

BESS   It's an asterism.

THOM   What's an asterism?

BESS   A group of stars.

THOM   So's a constellation.

BESS   Yes. Go on. The Winter Circle . . .

THOM   So, see Orion's Belt.

BESS   Uhuh.

THOM   Go down to the right . . . where his right foot would be.

BESS   His left foot.

THOM   To the right?

BESS   He's facing us.

THOM   Oh yeah. So his left foot. See that? That bright star is called Regal—*(correcting himself)* Rigel. Now go back to the belt.

BESS   Okay.

THOM   If you go straight across to your left . . . uh, yes—his right, your left—that's Sirius.

BESS   Seriously?

THOM grimaces playfully at BESS's joke.

THOM   And then it's almost a perfect circle: *(pointing out the stars)* Procyon. Castor and Pollux sort of together there on the upper left. Capella . . .

BESS	God bless you.
THOM	Aldebaran . . . and back to Regal—*Rigel*.
BESS	Regal's fine with me.

> *He tickles her.*

/ Ha, ha! Don't.

THOM	Clever bum. Am I boring you?
BESS	Are you kidding? I love this. *(shouting to the sky)* I—LOVE—THIS!!

> THOM *looks at* BESS *for a moment.*

THOM	Don't you wish sometimes you could just sail away?
BESS	Mmmm— Why?
THOM	I don't know. Expectations.

To spend the rest of my nights just . . . wandering. I'd like that.

> BESS *thinks about this.*

BESS	Not me.

Where's Virgo?

THOM	She's a snowbird: not back till the weather warms up.
BESS	I'm a Virgo.
THOM	When's your birthday?
BESS	September seventh.
THOM	I don't know any Virgos I don't think. What are you if you're a Virgo?
BESS	An analytical thinker.
THOM	Ahah.

BESS	Hard-working.
	Modest.
THOM	That's you.

BESS looks THOM in the eye.

BESS	A virgin.
THOM	I expect so.
BESS	They used to sacrifice virgins—know why?
THOM	I . . . could hazard a guess . . .
BESS	Because the gods want that power. Because what's inside me is so . . . volatile, so . . . potent, that . . . if the demons got hold of my soul it would be pure destruction.
THOM	Let's hope the gods get you instead.
BESS	Yeah! Then I'm pure . . . inspiration. Invention.
	A virgin is a *vessel* for creation.
THOM	How about that.
BESS	And heaven . . . Some say . . . heaven is . . . constantly having sex with virgins.

They look at each other for a tiny moment. Then back to the stars.

THOM	So, then . . . how might this . . . asterism . . . be used to . . . navigate, do you think?
BESS	You're Sirius . . . about this assignment.
THOM	I'm doing my best to stick to the task at hand.
BESS	*(answering his question)* By knowing where it rises and sets.
THOM	Yes. Rising in the southeast, it journeys westward through the night, and then sets in the southwest just before dawn. If you keep / those stars

BESS   I'm cold.

THOM   Here.

    He opens his coat and puts her inside it with him.

    If you keep / those stars

BESS   It's a beautiful sky. Our English sky.

THOM   Ours. Yes. Especially with the moon.

BESS   That's Jupiter, isn't it?

THOM   Jupiter, I meant. Mmhmm.

    She kisses him. He looks at her.

BESS   Are you comfortable with that?

THOM   No. I shouldn't be letting you—

    He kisses her. They look at each other. Then back out at the night.

BESS   What are the stars?

THOM   They're sparkly dots in the darkening sky; they're . . . like our sun: the hub of a solar system; they're fire, and radiation, and storms, and energy—pretty complex really. They're a puzzle we can put together so we don't get lost when we're sailing.

BESS   All that.

THOM   Uhuh.

BESS   I'm a star.

THOM   Are you.

BESS   Can I tell you a secret?

THOM   I'm . . . not sure / I

BESS   I get frightened.

THOM	Why?
BESS	Because inside I'm fire and radiation and storms. Big, nasty, violent storms.
THOM	You're fourteen.
BESS	And a puzzle.
THOM	We all are in a way.
BESS	But do you feel like you're an unstoppable force drawing everything in your path towards your life-sucking centre?
THOM	Not really.
BESS	I do. And I absorb it all.
THOM	I don't know how it is for girls.
BESS	We cover all that up. And what people see is the sparkly little dot.
THOM	You are luminous.
BESS	I dream of strange things.
THOM	Like?
BESS	What if you hate me for it?
THOM	I won't. Promise.
BESS	Being ravaged by ambitious men.
	Killing my stupid brother.
	Being King. Not Queen. King.
	Being dirty and wicked.
	I dream of those things.
	Am I still a star?
	Am I still a virgin then?
THOM	Maybe not in the eyes of the average person.

BESS	See, that's what scares me.
THOM	Don't be scared.
BESS	I want to be adored by average people.

HIDDEN MOTIVE TWO—JANUARY 20, 1549

In private. ASHLEY and ELEANOR continue.

ELEANOR	You think it was innocent?
ASHLEY	Do you have no memory of being a teenager? It's not easy. She has lots of . . . feelings.
ELEANOR	The women in her family have always had more *feelings* than they can control.
ASHLEY	*(adamant)* She's not like her mother.
ELEANOR	She's exactly like her mother: it starts with a little harmless narcissism, and before you know it she has no conscience. She'll have her Smeaton, her George, / her
ASHLEY	Her Bill.

This lands on ELEANOR and her reaction is instant.

ELEANOR	Stand up.
ASHLEY	You're making this personal, so why can't I?
ELEANOR	Keep this up. I dare you.
ASHLEY	I remember Bill Brereton: when you were working for Anne. You and the king's equerry, you / were
ELEANOR	Fair warning.
ASHLEY	I don't see why Bess's mother gets all the blame.

ELEANOR	Because women in her position are held to a higher standard. They need to understand their responsibility. He / was
ASHLEY	It's not like she overcame him physically.
ELEANOR	He Lost His Head!
ASHLEY	So did she! And now you're visiting the sins of the mother / upon the—
ELEANOR	Stand up.
ASHLEY	Judge and jury. Because her mom put the screw to your old boyfriend. You worried? That maybe Bess is his kid?
ELEANOR	Collateral damage, those men. You think Bess won't throw you to the wolves if it moves her one step closer to what she wants?
ASHLEY	She won't have to. I'm already here.
ELEANOR	STAND UP!!

ASHLEY *stands.*

	(*on a mission*) Thomas Seymour has blatantly disobeyed the Council's wishes and is thereby a threat to the kingdom. Encouraging his marriage to the princess is sedition.
ASHLEY	I haven't / been—
ELEANOR	That makes you a conspirator in an overthrow of the current administra / tion,
ASHLEY	Conspirator?
ELEANOR	complicit in a / coup,
ASHLEY	I may be / a lousy governess but—
ELEANOR	a facilitator of regime change,
ASHLEY	I have no interest in—
ELEANOR	and will see you arrested for treason / and

ASHLEY   Treason?!

ELEANOR   imprisoned in the tower / right

ASHLEY   Me?

ELEANOR   beside your eligible bachelor, and the girl who would be Queen.

ASHLEY   I'm looking out for— I'm taking care of that girl.

ELEANOR   So am I. Something in common.

Up on the crate.

ASHLEY climbs on the wooden box.

ASHLEY   I—

ELEANOR   Arms horizontal! At your sides!

ASHLEY   I won't talk. And it won't bring Bill back.

ELEANOR   Drop your head!

ASHLEY does. ELEANOR puts the bag over ASHLEY's head.

ASHLEY   Wait. I can't see. Are their nose holes in here?

ELEANOR   Lower your arms and the result will be extremely distasteful.

We need to know what we need to know.

ELEANOR leaves. A door slams tightly shut. ASHLEY stands in the silence.

ASHLEY   Hello?

Silence.

Hello?

Silence.

What do you need to know?

ASHLEY lets her arms relax slightly. An extremely loud warning buzzer is heard. She instantly raises her arms back up. The reality of her situation dawns on her:

Jesus Christ help me.

SHREDS—JANUARY 20, 1549

In public. It's raining. A woman with her hood up walks quickly by. A few moments later BESS appears with an umbrella up. She finds shelter and puts the umbrella down, shaking off the water. She looks around. She waits. The woman in the hood returns, looks around, joins her under the shelter.

MARY   I'm not here.

BESS   I know, but thanks for coming.

MARY   Now what is so gosh-darned urgent that we need a covert operation in the rain.

BESS   *(panicking)* They're so much better at this than me. Maybe I am just a child. They're so . . . intense, like . . . *(very close to her face)* right here.

MARY   / Uhuh.

BESS   I'm not going to get away with it. They'll arrest me. They'll have me killed. If Thom talks / it's all—

MARY   Just—clam up for one second, will you! There's no point in you— What is the point of you losing your noodle? It's a waste of your intelligence and a waste of my, my—well, a waste of something I don't have very much of apparently.

BESS   Really, Mary. I'm frightened.

MARY   Yuh, well, your head's not on the block just yet, little sister.

If you're a child you're no ordinary child. And, believe me, they have no idea what they're dealing with.

BESS   It's— Eleanor asked about that day in the garden.

MARY   *(this is not good)* Oh. Boy. And? You said?

BESS   What could I say?

MARY   Not the truth.

BESS   What is the truth?

MARY   That your pregnant stepmother held your arms behind your back while her husband cut your dress into a hundred pieces.

BESS   Yeah. Well, I didn't tell them that.

MARY   You lied?

BESS   *(worried)* No! But it's the first question I couldn't answer.

MARY   There is no answer to that question.

BESS   Right? Do *you* understand what happened that day?

MARY   I've / never—

BESS   Why? Why did Kate do that?

MARY   Because good people do weird shit.

BESS   But to *me*? Why would she do that to *me*?

MARY   It was for him.

BESS   For—for Thom. To—?

MARY   Excite him.

BESS   Oh.

MARY   Sexually.

BESS   Oh. I can't tell Ted and Eleanor that.

MARY   No.

BESS   What can I tell them?

      MARY reluctantly gets on board.

MARY   You tell them what you know: you were . . . wearing your black wool dress, right?

BESS   Two years official mourning.

MARY   And Kate and Thom were trying to snap you out of your grief, yes? They . . . thought you should break those old-fashioned rules: wearing black . . .

BESS   It was the wool: stifling! Stupid hot!

MARY   And teenagers smell.

BESS   *(surprised)* They do?

MARY   Wull . . . yeah.

BESS   You never told me that.

MARY   What, am I your mother now? There are things you should do. Ask Ashley.

BESS   Wow. I will.

MARY   *(back to the story)* So, Kate had given you a pretty cotton dress—

BESS   A pursie-man dress.

MARY   Hmh?

BESS   The colour. *(less confidently)* Pursie-man.

MARY   *(translating)* Persimmon.

BESS   Persimmon.

MARY   —But you were like: "No! I have to wear my black wool dress! It's only been six months!" So . . . they . . .

BESS   They . . . ?

MARY   I don't know: they assaulted you. How do we make that clean and good.

       MARY and BESS consider this.

BESS   *(a real question)* Do you think . . . ? Was it a game?

MARY   In the story or for real?

BESS   Yes.

MARY   Did it feel like a game?

BESS   It felt like something I should try to forget.

MARY   Rrrright then. You know what, poppet? We're never going to know why Kate did what she did. Did you love her?

BESS   Yes.

MARY   Did she love you?

BESS   Yes.

MARY   Then. That's what we know.

    And Eleanor and Ted? They / don't know—

BESS   They don't know anything, I don't think. They're just waiting for me to put my foot in it.

MARY   Yeah, well, don't put your foot in anything but a lavender bath.

BESS   Okay then.

    I'll, I'll say . . . it was a game.

MARY   Yeah. Thom and Kate were— *(idea!)* maybe they were tickling you.

BESS   That's—they could have been. We always played tickle.

MARY   There you go.

BESS   Normal family fun.

MARY	The title of your memoir.
BESS	Not funny.
MARY	Sí, mi hermana. *[Yes, my sister.]*
	You tell the tickle story to Ted and Eleanor.
	Okay?
BESS	Okay.
MARY	We done?
BESS	Yuh.
MARY	It's . . . good. I think it's good. Just don't fuck it up.
BESS	Okay.
MARY	Okay. Yo voy de aquí. *[I'm outta here.]*
	And just so we're clear, I'm not coming out again.
	Especially if it's raining.

> MARY *puts up her umbrella and goes.* BESS *takes a deep breath.*

IMPROPRIETY—JUNE 1548 / ASHLEY'S TORTURE—JANUARY 21, 1549 / EXILE—JUNE 1548 / INTERVIEW FOUR—JANUARY 21, 1549

> *At table.* ELEANOR *and* BESS. *There is a box with a lid on the table between them.*

ELEANOR	Katherine Parr—the woman you called *mother*—aided her husband in an act of sexual misconduct.
BESS	That's not what it was. I had real parents for the first time. We played together.

ELEANOR	"Normal family fun."
BESS	We laughed.
ELEANOR	*You* laughed. *They* laughed playing "Let's cut the dress off a child."
BESS	Nearly fifteen. And I had a slip on.
ELEANOR	. . . with a slip on . . . Kate holds your arms while Thomas cuts off your dress.
BESS	How many times do you have to say it?

BESS takes a drink of water.

ELEANOR	Do you regret it?
BESS	I—

BESS falters.

Why would I regret playing tickle?

ELEANOR	Do you have *any* feelings at all about the things that you've done?

BESS stands up to her own misgivings.

BESS	I loved Kate. She loved me. That's what we know.
ELEANOR	Did you love Thom?

BESS says nothing.

In the Chelsea garden, playing games: you were too young to know what you were feeling for Thom.

ELEANOR takes the lid off the box.

Even when he started coming to your bed.

BESS can see inside the box.

You're still too young. Right this minute. Do you know what you feel?

BESS   I don't—

ELEANOR takes a small teddy bear out of the box and sits it on the table.

We played tickle. Ashley knows. Ask her.

ELEANOR   We have.

This lands on BESS . . .

How do you think we found out?

. . . and a crack appears.

* * *

In private. ASHLEY stands on a wooden box as before: bag over her head and arms raised at her sides. She is disoriented by TED's voice coming from different speakers.

TED   Did you find the admiral in bed with the princess?

ASHLEY   And I yelled at him—!

TED   / Yes or no.

ASHLEY   —Are you kidding, I was / furious!

TED   So, "yes."

ASHLEY   I told him the Council would hear all about it. He swore at me, said he didn't care if the *entire parliament* saw what he was doing. Why would he say that if he'd done anything wrong?

TED   Did she lead him on?

ASHLEY   No! He was— *(stops herself)*

TED   What? He was what?

ASHLEY *(throwing* THOM *under the boat)* Taking advantage of a teenage girl.

TED A girl who had permission from you to set her own sexual
boundaries.

* * *

At bed. THOM *stands at the door in a nightshirt.* BESS *is
asleep.*

THOM Hey, sleepy head.

BESS Oh.

BESS appears from under the covers.

I'm not up yet.

THOM Are you getting up? I need to talk to you.

BESS I—I'm still in bed.

(giggle) Nice nightgown.

THOM Thanks.

BESS holds the covers up to her chin.

You know that letter I gave you?

BESS Which letter?

THOM In the book. The *Mary Rose.*

BESS Ancient history.

THOM I need you to know it wasn't a trifle. I meant what I said.

BESS What.

THOM All the things I said about you.

A moment.

I don't know what to do about you.

BESS   What do you mean?

THOM   I'm playing with fire.

A moment.

And what about Kate? What do we do about Kate?

BESS   We?

THOM   What do we do about the baby?

BESS   We, who? You mean . . . you and me?

THOM   No. Not you. I'll sort it out. I have to. I'll get it sorted out.

THOM goes to the bed. He sits on it.

* * *

ASHLEY and TED as before.

TED   And the queen? What did the queen think when she found her husband in bed with her daughter?

ASHLEY   No—you see? She wasn't *in bed* with him: stop putting words in my mouth.

ASHLEY's arms slacken, the buzzer sounds.

Aaargh—

TED   They were in the bed together.

ASHLEY   Kate knew it was nothing to be concerned about.

TED   And Bess? Did she encourage his advances?

ASHLEY   She, she . . . crawled back as far as she could into the bed.

TED   Did she elicit sexual relations?

ASHLEY   You're disgust / ing

TED   Were Elizabeth's sexual relations with the admiral the beginning of their *treasonous plot*?

* * *

> *THOM and* BESS *in the bed.* THOM *gets closer to* BESS.

THOM   Hey! Are you sleeping with your bear? A grown girl like you?

BESS   Yes.

THOM   Don't hide him. Let me see.

BESS   No, / he's

THOM   Come on. I want to see him.

BESS   Don't.

THOM   Come on, Bess. Show me Teddy.

> BESS *plays along.*

BESS   No. He's mine.

THOM   Tickle!

> THOM *starts to tickle* BESS. *She laughs. They play.*

BESS   Don't. Stop it.

THOM   I've got him.

BESS   No. Tho-om. Give him back.

THOM   You have to get him.

> THOM *hides the bear under the covers.*

Come find Teddy.

THOM dives under the covers. BESS follows him.

BESS   Aa! Noli me tangere! *[Touch thou not me.]*

THOM   What's that, Italian?

BESS   It's Latin.

BESS holds out the bear.

Ha, hah! I got him back!

THOM appears from under the sheets. BESS tackles him play-fully just as there is a noise behind her. THOM looks over BESS's shoulder.

THOM   Shit.

ASHLEY, from the crate:

ASHLEY   / Kate—

THOM leaps from the bed.

THOM
& BESS   Kate.

* * *

ASHLEY and TED as before.

ASHLEY   *(Kate)* —didn't make a big deal of it. They never did any-thing in that bed!

TED   And yet, after that day, the queen and the admiral came *together* to wake the princess.

ASHLEY   Yes. They came together.

TED   And plans were immediately made to send Bess away.

ASHLEY   We couldn't stay.

TED	Thom stayed. Pretty obvious that Kate blamed Bess for seducing her husband.
ASHLEY	That's not—
TED	Bess was sent away!

* * *

In private. BESS *and* THOM. BESS *is beside herself in tears, guilt, and panic.*

THOM	It'll be okay. Kate loves you.
BESS	And then she catches me in bed with her husband!
THOM	You were not in bed with me.
BESS	I was *in the bed*!
THOM	That's a totally different thing. You need—you absolutely need to make that distinction.

PARRY enters, a little pale.

PARRY	You're okay.
BESS	Stop saying that.
PARRY	Kate's gone to bed.
THOM	*(that's odd)* She just got up.
PARRY	Ashley's with her. She's having some pain.
THOM	With the baby?
BESS	Pain with the / baby?
THOM	I'll go see / her.
BESS	Don't / go!
PARRY	She's lying down.

BESS	I'm going to be sick.
	(to PARRY) Really, Parry, I think I'm going to be sick.
PARRY	I'll get something.
	PARRY goes.
BESS	*(to THOM)* Can't you hold me?
THOM	You know I can't.
BESS	She's sending me away.
THOM	Just to Hatfield.
BESS	Hatfield Mars.
THOM	It's not a punishment.
BESS	That's what she said.
	PARRY comes back with a wastebasket.
PARRY	Put your head over the bucket. Try to breathe.
	PARRY pours a tumbler of water, leaves it on the table near BESS.
THOM	Kate's protecting you.
BESS	She said it would protect her.
	(to THOM) And you.
PARRY	*(to THOM)* Not sure why you need protecting.
BESS	Oh God . . .
	BESS puts her head back over the wastebasket.
THOM	It's clear now at least. You'll go away.
BESS	Now you can't wait to be rid of me. The things you said to me just now—
THOM	Kate and I are having a child—
BESS	So, am I a true match for you or not?

PARRY   / Match?

THOM   No, I—

BESS   No? Is that true? / What's true?

THOM   I mean—

PARRY   What did you say to her?

BESS   *(to THOM)* You don't even know yourself.

THOM   I'm sorry I said that.

BESS   You're—what— / Sorry?

THOM   Please, / Bess—

BESS   *(to PARRY)* You want to know what else he / said?

THOM   —we'll all get past this.

BESS   I *was* past it. I was just past the last time.

PARRY   The time you sent your letters out to three lucky
          bachelorettes . . .

THOM   That / was a completely

BESS   . . . and then, in my bed just now you said that you— And
          you can just—? And I've only *now* got past the last time!!

          PARRY gives BESS the tumbler of water.

PARRY   Messy-one— You / need to

THOM   You need to go away.

          *BESS drinks the tumbler of water. Something changes deep
          in BESS.*

BESS   *(to PARRY)* I'm okay now. I'll be okay.

          PARRY takes the wastebasket off.

THOM   I'll send word to you.

BESS   What, to tell me how your baby's doing?

THOM	Don't you want to know?
BESS	I'll find out from the queen.

BESS looks THOM in the eye.

(willfully) I'm going to give your baby girl such a whack when I see her for giving our Kate / so much grief.

THOM	Girl . . . ?
BESS	*(composing herself)* Please tell Kate that Ashley and Parry and I will be at Hatfield praying for a safe / delivery.
THOM	You think it's a girl?
BESS	Tell her I'll write soon.

* * *

BESS sits at one end of the table. ELEANOR is walking the perimeter.

ELEANOR	Kate didn't blame him: she blamed you. Sent you away from the man you were smitten with.

You must see it as justice then that she met a gruesome end.

BESS becomes instantly disquieted.

BESS	Stop talking.
ELEANOR	I was there. As Kate was dying. She mentioned you.

Trying to stay on top of things, BESS stands up and looks for TED.

BESS	Where's Ted? He said he'd be back by now.
ELEANOR	She grabbed my arm so hard: "The kinder I am to them, the more horrible they are to me." Screamed it, almost. Who's "they"? Did Kate mean you, do you think: "the

more horrible they are to me"? Was she putting the pieces together by then? She must have known that as soon as she died you'd jump in to take her place.

BESS   Guard!

ELEANOR   Laughing at her, she said. That poor woman: dying, with her newborn daughter beside her. And you laughed. You and Thomas. Is that what was torturing her?

Elizabeth! I'm asking you!

BESS   We're not on the record!

A buzzer is heard in the distance.

What's that?

ELEANOR   Did she figure out your plans?

BESS   Plans to do—what's that noise?

ELEANOR   Thom sat with Kate then. Held his baby girl. I left. A private goodbye. A woman who loved her husband very much.

BESS thinks she sees TED coming.

BESS   *(calling)* Ted?

(back to ELEANOR) Oh. I'm gonna be sick.

ELEANOR   I can certainly understand why neither of you could show your face at the funeral.

* * *

The scenes overlap now: ASHLEY and TED, BESS and ELEANOR.

TED   Why did neither Elizabeth nor the admiral attend the queen's funeral.

ASHLEY   Bess was—

TED   Pregnant?

        BESS   I'm gonna barf, okay?! Seriously! I'm ill!

        ELEANOR   Were you hiding from the Council?

ASHLEY   She was sick.

TED   Morning sickness?

ASHLEY   Menstrual cramps.

TED   She was vomiting.

ASHLEY   She sometimes does.

TED   And that kept her from *her mother's* funeral?

        BESS   I was extremely distressed: physically, emotionally.

        ELEANOR   And yet, within the month . . . Ashley suggested you marry Thom, and he kept on Kate's household staff, awaiting the arrival of his new bride.

        BESS   I said no.

TED   Were you planning Bess's marriage to the admiral?

ASHLEY   I-it's complicated.

TED   It is *treason* to make any marital arrangement for an heir to the throne without the Council's permission.

        BESS   The Council would be happy if I never married anyone at all! Let alone someone important. / They want to tuck me away at Hatfield so people forget all about me: just another girl doing needlepoint.

ASHLEY   The Council wants to see her barefoot, pregnant, and shacked up with some Kraut. Thomas is an eligible peer. *The* eligible peer. He was King Henry's choice, not mine.

	TED	That's the first I've heard of it.

TED   That's the first I've heard of it.

ASHLEY   Then you're out of the loop.

TED   What was her response to your suggestion of marriage?

ASHLEY   No.

    ELEANOR   You said no?

    BESS   Yes.

    ELEANOR   You didn't write him letters?

    BESS   No.

TED   Did she tell you she wanted to write him?

ASHLEY   *I* told her she *should* write him.

TED   You suggested they continue their liaison?

ASHLEY   They'd lived in the same house for two years!

    ASHLEY's arms slacken. A buzzer sounds.

    I can't! I can't!

TED   Did you suggest they continue their liaison?!

ASHLEY   I thought it would lift her spirits. To share her grief.

    BESS   I was mourning Kate's death. So was he.

    ELEANOR   / So you wrote him.

TED   So she wrote him.

ASHLEY & BESS   No.

ASHLEY   She didn't want it to look like she was chasing him.

TED   / Chasing him! See?

    ELEANOR   You were chasing him.

    BESS   No!

ASHLEY   All the straight women in England were chasing him!

    ELEANOR   Sending / secret messages.

TED   Did you convey secret messages from the princess to the admiral telling him to lay low?

The arms slacken, a buzzer sounds.

ASHLEY
& BESS   No!

ASHLEY   There were no secrets.

    ELEANOR   But you'd been so close? Such a happy family?

      BESS   I'm really not well.

TED   *(a new thought)* Was evidence of their correspondence *destroyed?*

ASHLEY   The princess was very careful not to arouse suspicion.

TED   *(bingo)* Because she was hatching a plot!

ASHLEY   Damn it—not that kind of suspicion—

The arms slacken, a buzzer sounds.

I can't think straight with this fucking bag over my head!

Silence.

Hello?

Silence.

Oh God.

* * *

TED enters with a plate of sandwiches. BESS vomits into her hanky.

TED   Oh / dear.

ELEANOR   Well.

BESS   Ted! Ted: I want her out!

TED   Eleanor? She's here to protect you.

ELEANOR   I'll get something to clean you up.

ELEANOR goes.

* * *

ASHLEY alone.

ASHLEY   Ted?

Silence.

* * *

TED puts the plate down and helps BESS, who is very agitated.

BESS   I won't tell you anything if she's here!

TED   *(calming her)* Easy now. What is it—what is it you have to tell me?

BESS	Eleanor's been upsetting me by talking about Kate!
TED	No, no, no. You're okay now.

* * *

ELEANOR is now directly beside ASHLEY, though ASHLEY cannot see her.

ASHLEY	Ted? Hello?
ELEANOR	*(precisely)* Did / you collude—
ASHLEY	*(jumping out of her skin)* Damn / you!
ELEANOR	Did the princess form an alliance with the admiral that was a threat to King Edward?
ASHLEY	I peed. I just peed my pants! How on earth could any man love you?
ELEANOR	Answer the question or you'll stand here for another hour!!
ASHLEY	She was a teenager who had a crush on her handsome uncle. Father. Shit, you know what I mean! He was built, and mysterious, and a great fucking dancer. He just happened to show her tenderness and love, something she didn't have for most of her young life.

If I ever spoke to her about marrying him, it was *my* error in judgment. But she didn't seriously consider it. *I* was incompetent. *It's my fault,* and she relied on me. Please!!! Can I—I can't hold my arms up anymore!!

* * *

TED stands opposite BESS.

TED   We don't have to talk about Kate.

BESS   This has nothing to do with Kate dying!

TED   Did you have breakfast?

BESS   I loved Kate!

A buzzer is heard in the distance. BESS jumps.

Tell me what that noise is!

TED   Have a sandwich. Cheese!

BESS   This has nothing to do with Kate dying!

TED   No, no, no: of course, of course.

What has nothing to do with Kate dying?

COMMANDER—NOVEMBER 1548

In public. It's raining. A man with his hood up walks quickly by. A few moments later BESS appears with an umbrella up. She finds shelter and puts the umbrella down, shaking off the water. She looks around. She waits. The man in the hood returns, looks around, joins her under the shelter.

THOM   Hi, Bess.

BESS   Hi, Thom.

THOM   I did what you said.

BESS   Is Eddie taking it?

THOM	Each time I see him he wants more.
BESS	He's relying on you now. That's good.
THOM	Ted's a cheapskate. No allowance? For the king?
BESS	And you talked with Eddie about making you Protector?
THOM	I did. But he said he's not comfortable sticking himself between Ted and me.
BESS	You've gotta get custody of Eddie. Get Ted out.
THOM	I will. And I'll be a great protector until you're—

THOM reaches for BESS; she stops his hand.

BESS	Too public.
THOM	Let's just take Eddie.
BESS	Take him? No. It needs to stay clean. And good.
THOM	Clean or good: it's still treason.
BESS	It's not treason.
THOM	Your dad chose Eddie.
BESS	He didn't choose Ted.
	Separate Eddie and Ted, they have nothing: Eddie's not ready to be king, and Ted . . . is not a cognate.
THOM	Sorry?
BESS	His father didn't wear a crown.
THOM	My father.
BESS	Yes.

A moment.

THOM	What about Mary?
BESS	Catholic.
THOM	Right.

A moment.

BESS   The people will support me.

THOM   *Us.*

BESS   Yes. *We* have a legitimate claim to the throne, and together we'll prove ourselves worthy.

THOM   Together. Okay.

A moment.

BESS   You've made contact with Sharington?

THOM   He's been putting money in an account for me.

BESS   And the pirates?

THOM   Assembling in the southwest. As long as we pay them, they'll do what we ask.

BESS   Good then. Money, troops, and the trust of the people. All we need is to get Eddie away from Ted.

THOM   And then . . . you and I will—

THOM reaches for BESS again. She takes him by the wrist.

BESS   Not here. Not now. Our time will come.

End of Act One.

ACT TWO
SILHOUETTE—FEBRUARY 21, 1549

In private. We see the silhouette of a young woman dressing. She puts her hands on her belly. Is she pregnant? Is her belly protruding just a bit? She turns. Oh. No. Maybe she's not pregnant. Is it a trick of the light? If she just turns back we can know for certain. But she's slipped on a dress, and it's now impossible to say. She's just a teenaged girl heading out into her day.

OFF THE RECORD—FEBRUARY 21, 1549

At table. BESS *sits at one end of the table. After a few moments,* TED *enters.*

BESS   Ted!

TED   Hi, honey.

     TED *sees that* BESS *is alone.*

     Where's Eleanor?

BESS   I don't care.

TED   Oh. Dear then. Not to worry. I'll wait outside.

BESS   No. Can I talk to you?

TED   You know we can't do that.

BESS   There are things I can't say in front of Eleanor.

TED   Really, Bess? Like what?

BESS   Do you think I'm a bad person?

TED   Why on earth would you say that?

BESS   Do you think I'm lying?

TED   Have you told me the whole truth?

BESS   You're answering my questions with questions.

TED   *(a joke)* Don't you like my questions?

        BESS *is not amused.*

BESS   Nothing's funny right now.

TED   Oh shoot, I'm sure. Go on then.

BESS   I feel like you're blaming me for what Thom did.

TED   We just need to know how much you were involved.

BESS   You said I was innocent.

TED   Are you?

BESS   You don't treat me like I am. Everything that happened to me is called into question. And now . . .

TED   Now what?

BESS   New rumours.

TED   What rumours?

BESS   That I'm being held on charges. That I'm locked in the Tower.

TED   That's ludicrous. You're free to go.

BESS	And more.
TED	Good grief, how people talk.
BESS	"Locked up and knocked up."
TED	They're saying *that*?
BESS	By the lord admiral.
TED	That is just dreadful.
BESS	Shameful.
TED	Slanderous, I'd say.
BESS	I worry that this is the beginning of something.
TED	Of what?
BESS	That the questions aren't about Thom, they're about me: my integrity, my . . . reputation, my . . . inherent . . . nature. That you're putting me on trial.
TED	See: that's the problem, I think.
BESS	What is?
TED	Ha, ha! You're too smart for your own good.
BESS	Some people are threatened by me. So I need all my wits about me, don't you think? I can't possibly be too smart for my own good.

A moment.

Are you charging me with involvement in Thom's plot?

TED	You're a witness. That's all.
BESS	Then arrange for me to see Eddie.
TED	What does it have to do with Eddie?
BESS	If I go to court and show everyone there that I'm freely walking around and obviously *not* in a family way, then . . .

TED   Then . . . ?

BESS   I stop the rumours. Clear my name. That's important to me. To make it clean. Make it good.

TED   I will absolutely see what I can do.

BESS   Thanks, Ted. The public need to know I had nothing to do with Thom's plot.

TED   Oh, not to worry: Thom has told us over and over again that you know nothing. Isn't that right? Nothing about Sharington . . . ? The money . . . ? The pirates . . . ?

CRASH—JANUARY 14, 1549

In public. A corridor. THOM *sees* TED *and starts to book it in the opposite direction.* TED *catches him. Stops him. They strain to keep this conversation from being overheard.*

TED   They searched Sharington's house!

THOM   They did / what?

TED   They got a warrant and searched Sharington's house. Guess what they found?

THOM   How would I / know?

TED   Bank statements! He left bank statements! You didn't think to open a foreign account?

THOM   Me—?

TED   They're going to come for you now. They have evidence Sharington's been funnelling funds to you. If you tell me why, I can help.

THOM   *(trying to leave)* It's none of your business.

TED	*(stopping him)* Thom!
THOM	I don't exactly pull in a salary like yours, how's that. Whatever they say, it was all legal.
TED	Come. On. Two million pounds— Two / million?
THOM	Nothing to do with / me.
TED	We're talking about comb-over Bill Sharington here.
THOM	He's been cooking the books for years.
TED	You asked him to price out wages and keep for ten thousand men.
THOM	/ He told—?
TED	What have you got yourself involved in?
THOM	Did you make him say that?
TED	Me?
THOM	No, you sicced Eleanor on him.
TED	Two million pounds. Ten thousand men. Can you see how the Council might imagine a *plot* based on that information?
THOM	And did Sharington say what I was gonna do with all the money and men?
TED	He wouldn't say.
THOM	There is no *plot*. That's why. Not even one you can imagine.
TED	Then why are you meeting with Bess / when she's
THOM	/ Oh, for the love of—
TED	in town to see the / king.
THOM	Who else have you been torturing?
TED	She's behind this. Is she? Tell me! I'll deal with her.
THOM	/ She

TED	Have you been duped by her?
THOM	Duped?
TED	You see, that's what I'm imagining: you marry Bess, bump off Eddie and Mary—
THOM	/ Bump them off—?
TED	and when she's Queen you sit as her consort.
THOM	Are you hearing / yourself—?
TED	If I can put that together you think the Council won't? Did she suggest the two of you—stop and think—did she *ever* discuss making a bid for the throne?

THOM says nothing.

	Pleeease listen to me: little Eddie's sisters are the enemy. If his *uncle* marries one of them—if he's colluding with one of them—that's a threat. The king will see it as a threat.
THOM	The king? Or the protector.
TED	If this is Elizabeth's idea we need to expose her!
THOM	*(adamant)* I haven't been duped.

There is a taught stillness between them.

TED	Come to Council then. Give us a rational explanation for this Sharington business.

THOM asserts his only power.

THOM	Sorry. The timing isn't good for me.
TED	I can't believe— For your king you won't—?
THOM	For my country. I won't.
TED	Right. Well. Keep your coat on then. It's damp in the Tower. And cold.

BURN—JANUARY 16, 1549

At bed. BESS *is sleeping.* THOM *stands in the doorway for a time. He's drunk. He walks to the bed and puts his hand over* BESS's *mouth. She struggles and then calms as she sees it's* THOM.

THOM   Hi, Bess.

BESS   Hi, Thom.

Oh. You smell like booze.

Nothing happens.

You're in my bed. In the night.

THOM *puts his head in* BESS's *lap.*

THOM   The Council wants a different kind of man for you. Not a mere mortal, no: not me; they don't want me. I'm not good enough for you.

I wasn't good enough for Kate. I loved Kate. Kate loved Henry.

THOM *looks at* BESS *and sees a woman.*

I love you.

BESS   What's happened?

THOM   I've been set up. I've been *duped*!

BESS   Shhhh. Someone will come.

THOM   I don't care. Let them find me.

I love you. I'm a fool. Ask my brother.

THOM *looks at* BESS *and sees a child.*

Tickle?

THOM starts to tickle BESS. BESS backs away. THOM pulls her close.

It's okay, it's okay. I just want to hold you.

BESS allows this, but doesn't relax entirely.

Sharington's behind bars. The Council is adding it up: one, two, me, you.

BESS   Me?

THOM   I'm sorry, I messed up. Kiss me. I will never tell them it was your idea.

BESS   What did Ted / say?

THOM   Shhhh. Never, never. I owe you a promise. I've broken too many.

You look so young right now.

BESS   You won't tell / them

THOM   Cross my heart and hope to die. Ha, ha! Hope to die and probably will!

BESS   Does the Council know / what

THOM   *(in a panic now, whispering)* Oh God. I don't want to go to the Tower.

(anger now) I'm not going to the fucking Tower.

Will they guarantee me that it's just for questioning? No.

(fear now) I won't get out of the Tower. People like me don't get out of the Tower.

Hold me, okay? Here.

THOM puts BESS's arms around him.

(still whispering) Come on, Bess! Hold me!

BESS engages a little more, but she is vigilant.

I'm scared.

BESS Talk to Ted.

THOM Hah!

BESS He's your brother.

THOM Do you trust your sister?

THOM's anger begins to fuel him.

Fratricide: kill your brother. That's from the Latin.

Someone told Ted about Sharington. Did you set me up?

BESS Ted will keep you out of the Tower.

THOM He won't have to. I'm taking his title.

THOM takes out a knife.

I'm gonna do it tonight.

BESS Do what?

THOM I'm gonna get Eddie.

BESS And do what with him?

THOM You're the one who said—I know what I'm doing! You think
I don't know what I'm doing?

What do you know? You're a *child*.

BESS I'm / not—

THOM I got the money; I got the troops; I got all the things you
asked for.

Fuck Henry. Fuck Ted. Fuck you. I've got the power!

BESS No, Thom—

THOM *(adamantly convincing her)* Yes, Bess. I'll be the protector of
Eddie. I'll be the protector of you.

Virgin power? *(protecting her)* You won't need it: I've got what it takes.

> THOM *kisses* BESS. *She pushes him away.*

What?

BESS   I don't want to.

THOM   Why? Because I smell?

> THOM *moves toward* BESS.

BESS   *(trying to contain him)* Thom, don't—

> THOM *brandishes the knife.*

THOM   I'll put this knife in anyone who lays hands on me.

> THOM *forces himself on* BESS.
>
> *We hear the sound of a barking dog, then a shot, and a whimper. An alarm is raised. The sound of shouting and running feet.*

WHITEWASHING—JANUARY 17, 1549

> *In private.* MARY *and* ASHLEY *enter.*

MARY   What are you thinking? The middle of the night!

ASHLEY   Thom's been arrested.

MARY   Yeah. My father'll be dancing in his grave.

ASHLEY   We / thought—

MARY   The whole court is in lockdown! Now don't you dare tell me you dragged me out of the comfort of my bed because my stupid sister is worried about that worm.

ASHLEY   / It was—

MARY	Seymours: they come across as totally pleasant people, but you scratch the surface and boom!—they are fucked up, that family. And our little Bess, well, isn't she just drawn to the weird ones.
ASHLEY	/ There's—
MARY	Oh for pity's sake. *You're* the adults here. You're the ones who are supposed to be advising her. It's neither my place, my obligation, nor my interest.
ASHLEY	We're a little out of our depth.
MARY	Why doesn't that surprise me.

PARRY enters with BESS. She's wrapped in a blanket and drinking from a mug. MARY immediately sees there's something wrong.

BESS	*(to ASHLEY)* Parry made me cocoa.
ASHLEY	Parry's a good egg.
MARY	What happened to her?

PARRY gets BESS a chair.

PARRY	Here. Sit down, little pumpkin.
MARY	What.
PARRY	*(to BESS)* Need a cushion?
BESS	No.
MARY	Tell me— What?

MARY stares at BESS. BESS meets her gaze head on.

Thom's been arrested.

BESS	We heard.
MARY	For trying to take Eddie.
BESS	Uhuh.

MARY	He had a gun.
BESS	He didn't have that when he was here.
MARY	When he was here.
BESS	Uhuh.
MARY	And was he . . . just dropping by? Here? Without a gun?
BESS	He had a knife.
MARY	A knife.
BESS	In my room.
MARY	Earlier. Tonight.
BESS	Before he went to get Eddie.
PARRY	We'll take her to Ted; we just / thought
MARY	*(precisely, to PARRY)* You can't go to Ted.

(to BESS) What did he . . . do? With the knife. |
ASHLEY	We thought we should run it by you / first.
MARY	*(to ASHLEY and PARRY)* You can't go to Ted.
PARRY	Who do / we—?
MARY	*(to BESS)* Is there a . . . correlation maybe? Between Thom being here and . . . the Eddie thing?
BESS	I-I don't know how much to tell / you.
MARY	Everything! Every. Little. Thing. I'll make sure he hangs by his—

(to ASHLEY and PARRY) Maybe if these *GENIUSES* had been doing their *JOB*, an innocent girl wouldn't have quite so much to tell me about what happened in her bedroom with that asshole and a knife!! |
| ASHLEY | You're sure we shouldn't go to Ted? |

MARY   *(sharply)* You will not go to Ted, okay! There's no reason to go to Ted. Word gets out that her . . . international trading potential has been . . . compromised and that's it. Future? No future. No marriage. No cute little kiddies to ride on the pony.

       MARY goes to BESS and pats her on the arm.

       Look. I'll be nice to you later. Swear. But I need to know how Thom being here relates to the dead fucking dog.

BESS   *(squirming)* I-I don't know how much / to tell you

MARY   Just. Start. I'll determine how long you drone on.

       BESS composes herself.

BESS   When father brought us back into the line of succession—

MARY   Bess.

BESS   What.

MARY   It's three a.m. Is there not a more recent entry in your diary that might serve as a starting point?

       BESS thinks.

BESS   Matilda.

MARY   Matilda?

BESS   Remember? Queen School Lesson Twelve: Matilda, Roman Empress, *almost* Queen.

MARY   What about her?

BESS   She had a legitimate claim to the throne.

MARY   That doesn't mean she got to sit in it.

BESS   The king didn't name an heir. He just made sure there were a bunch of strong candidates and when he died they were left to fight it out.

MARY   Where are we going with this?

BESS	They just had to prove themselves worthy by showing their strength to lead. Matilda was strong, smart, capable.
MARY	*(getting impatient)* She never sat on the throne! A *man* sat on the throne.
BESS	But Matilda had a legitimate claim . . .
PARRY	. . . had money, troops, political will . . .
MARY	*(dawn lights on MARY)* Oh. Boy.

> *A moment.*

> The crown belongs to Eddie.

PARRY	Eddie's a pawn for Ted.
MARY	And after Eddie there's me.
ASHLEY	Religion.
PARRY	Old school.

> *A moment.*

MARY	Then . . . so then. Comes. *You.*

> *A moment.*

PARRY	There's been a plan.
MARY	Shut. Up. Do Not Tell Me Anything Else. No details, you understand? It's not worth my life to be mixed up in this.

> *MARY goes to leave.*

BESS	Mary—
MARY	I'm not here. I never was.
BESS	Eddie will kill me, won't he. Can they kill a princess?
MARY	You think I'm sticking around to see how this turns out?!

> *She starts to leave again.*

BESS	Maryyyy?!

MARY His life or yours! What would you do? What would *I* do?!

BESS Don't be mean.

MARY If a *cognate* is knee deep in a coup?

PARRY *(not good news)* He has an *obligation* to kill you.

MARY And I wouldn't blame him if / he did.

BESS Don't be mean! Not now.

MARY You're trying to depose your own brother and you're asking *me* not to be / *mean*?

BESS Something horrible happened to me!!

MARY You've not exactly been the image of modesty.

ASHLEY *(adamant) That* was not her fault.

BESS Don't hurt me more!

MARY Fine. I take back that last part.

Holy crow! How did you plan to deal with me?

BESS I wasn't worried about you.

MARY Oh, that makes me feel a lot better.

(the Catch-22) And until you *kill* me I am *responsible* for you!

BESS You promised Father.

MARY Promises, promises.

(working it out) So, that cretin was part of your *plot* to usurp the throne—am I warm?—but something went inexplicably wrong: a . . . a . . . *series of events* in your bedroom, yes?

PARRY He was never meant to—

ASHLEY We had no idea about the gun.

BESS Or the knife.

MARY	Well, now they have *him*, they will certainly come for *you*. And your sidekicks.
PARRY	Us?
MARY	*(to PARRY)* You first.
PARRY	*(to ASHLEY)* This has gone side / ways.
MARY	And they'll start making shit up if there isn't a plausible story that you all agree on.
ASHLEY	We can straighten it out.
MARY	*(to BESS) You* can straighten it out. *You* need to be the heart of the story.
BESS	I don't feel well.
MARY	I'm very sorry about that. I really am.
	(clapping her hands like a football coach) Let's go! Let's go! What's your next move?
BESS	I . . . *(appealing for help)* Ashley . . . ?
MARY	No! You! Consider it a test of your "legitimate claim."
	BESS treads carefully.
BESS	The . . . the . . . *series of events* . . . in question . . . is a scandal. Isn't it.
MARY	It certainly has that potential.
BESS	And the . . . *series of events* . . . that I brought about . . .
ASHLEY	You did not bring it about.
BESS	that . . . *series of events* . . . can ruin me.
MARY	Ted and Eleanor will try take you down. That's their job. They'll create a version of Elizabeth Tudor that suits their agenda.

BESS	So . . . wait, then: can, can I create a version of Elizabeth Tudor that suits *my* agenda?
MARY	What is your agenda?
BESS	To clear my name. My reputation.
MARY	I'd bet the farm on it. Sheep and all.

BESS sees a pinprick of light at the end of the tunnel.

BESS	Okayyy. And as for the . . . *series of events* . . . well, no one gets to know about that unless I want them to.
	(on the horse now) What do I tell Ted and Eleanor?
MARY	They smell lies? It deepens their resolve.
BESS	So: no truth, no lies.
MARY	Welcome to life at the top.
BESS	I'll confess—*we'll* confess—
PARRY	"We'll" . . . ?
BESS	. . . the facts.
PARRY	Confess?
ASHLEY	Our *actual* involvement, yes?
MARY	No more.
BESS	They have no proof of anything more.
MARY	They have to have something if they arrested Thom.
ASHLEY	They have witnesses. Me. Parry.
MARY	Eee—that's a drag.
ASHLEY	They'll torture, won't they.
PARRY	They'll— That's not good. I'm not good with pain. I / can't
ASHLEY	*(adamantly, to PARRY)* You will do whatever is necessary for our little / girl.

PARRY	But you know / me. I can't
ASHLEY	You'll do what's right.
PARRY	But / torture—
BESS	Parry.
PARRY	Yuh. Okay. Yuh.
BESS	I'm innocent.
ASHLEY & PARRY	*(to BESS)* You're innocent.
MARY	And when Thom talks?
BESS	*(intuiting)* He won't.
MARY	Let me dream for just a second that he will.
BESS	*(bolstering her instinct)* Neither of us will tell.

A moment.

MARY	Alea iacta est. *[The die is cast.]*

Agree to the same set of facts. Don't speak about anything more than that. And never off the record, you hear?

BESS	Never off the record.
PARRY	They can drag me behind horses till dead.
MARY	Yeah . . . be careful what you wish for.

(to ASHLEY and PARRY) You two buzz off now and give me a moment with my sister before you never saw me.

ASHLEY and PARRY go. The sisters are silent for a moment.

So? The series of events.

BESS	He hurt me.
MARY	Maybe I can swing the axe.
BESS	Bruises. Here—

BESS begins lifting her gown to show. MARY *instantly averts her eyes.*

MARY   God. No. Don't. Show.

Why, though. Why did he do that?

BESS   Remember the dances at Chelsea?

MARY   Never invited.

BESS   I would blush when he took my hand . . .

The fire. Under my skin.

I would blush.

I don't know why he did this.

MARY   Is there evidence? That you conspired with him?

BESS   I didn't. I set him up.

MARY   You—?

BESS   I planned it. He did the job.

MARY   Hold on, hold on, hold on: give me a second to unpack this little suitcase.

BESS   I don't know how much to tell / you.

MARY   Oh for Pete's sake.

BESS   *(the plan)* I would be Queen, Thom would be Lord Protector, and after a suitable amount of time . . .

MARY   You'd charge him with treason. *(shaking her head)* Ha! Same old, same old. But you know that he'll . . .

BESS says nothing.

Yes, you know. You want him to . . .

The implications of this dawn on MARY.

Wow. "Don't be mean."

BESS	He's a user. And it doesn't even faze him.
MARY	He's spry, all right. But your work here is impressive.
BESS	As if a girl my age isn't yare. Isn't ready.
MARY	Apparently you're yare.
BESS	I *know* when things are wrong.
MARY	This, we share.

> *MARY looks directly at BESS.*

Did you plan to *kill* Eddie?

BESS	No!
MARY	I come next. Before you.
BESS	Yes.
MARY	Will I ever be able to trust you?
BESS	I'm your sister.

PARRY'S TORTURE / INTERVIEW FIVE—
FEBRUARY 28, 1549

> *In private. PARRY lies head downward on an inverted table.*
> *His face is covered by a towel. ELEANOR stands over him,*
> *gripping the towel around his neck. PARRY is drowning.*
> *ELEANOR removes the towel. PARRY chokes and sputters.*

ELEANOR	Why did you run when you saw the officers coming?
PARRY	*(choke)* I was frightened.
ELEANOR	Why did you say "We've been caught"?
PARRY	I— *(choke, choke)*
ELEANOR	Because you were guilty.

PARRY	Of what? Guilty of what?
ELEANOR	Why did you say "I wish I had never been born"?
PARRY	Guilty of what?
ELEANOR	Answer the question!!
PARRY	*(sputter)* Because I knew you were going to bring me here.
ELEANOR	You met with Thomas Seymour on several / occasions—
PARRY	We're business / associates.
ELEANOR	—in your position as Elizabeth's accountant.
PARRY	Yes. We met.
ELEANOR	You oversaw budgets for / the coup.
PARRY	I oversaw— The coup?!
ELEANOR	Was the plan to combine their land holdings in the south-west in order to stage an insurgence?
PARRY	I-I don't understand the question.

> *ELEANOR places the towel over PARRY's face and pours water onto the towel. PARRY drowns for a few seconds. ELEANOR removes the towel. PARRY chokes and sputters.*

ELEANOR	*(pedantically)* Each parcel of land in this country comes with an affinity of persons to defend that land. Did Elizabeth suggest swapping her current properties for holdings closer to the admiral's in order to establish a unified fighting force?
PARRY	He asked for reports.
ELEANOR	At her bidding?
PARRY	*(confused)* She doesn't need reports; it's her land.
ELEANOR	Are you getting smart with me?!
PARRY	No! I'm not smart! I promise!

ELEANOR	Did you and the admiral discuss exchanging the letters patent on her land?
PARRY	We discussed the patents . . .
ELEANOR	Yes. At her bidding.
PARRY	NO! That's not what—
ELEANOR	You just said you did!
PARRY	But she didn't seriously consider it.
	I'm not good at this! I can't remember!!
ELEANOR	Then you'll remember tomorrow.
PARRY	*(blubber)* Oh God—
ELEANOR	*(moving on)* Did Elizabeth know about the money accrued from Sharington's bank?
PARRY	I don't think so. *(seeing the towel coming)* No! No!

ELEANOR places the towel over PARRY's face and pours water onto the towel. PARRY drowns for a few seconds. ELEANOR removes the towel. PARRY chokes and sputters.

ELEANOR	Did she know of the admiral's association with pirates on the Isles of Scilly?
PARRY	Scilly? Pirates?
ELEANOR	You think this is a joke?!
PARRY	No I— *(choke)* It's not funny. I just don't understand!

ELEANOR places the towel over PARRY's face and pours water onto the towel. PARRY drowns for a few seconds. ELEANOR removes the towel. PARRY chokes and sputters.

(the agreed-upon statement) I participated in unauthorized accounting procedures: is that good? She relied on me. *I* was incompetent. It's *my fault.*

ELEANOR   *(putting this together with ASHLEY's statement)* What did you say?

PARRY   It was *my* error in judgment. *(unsure now)* It's my fault?

ELEANOR   Damn you.

PARRY   *(a last-ditch attempt)* Look, I'll give you all my jewellery: you want my gold chain? My rings? *(choke, choke, sputter, blubber, choke)*

> *ELEANOR removes the towel and restraints and normalizes the room. PARRY is shivering now, and weeping.*

           I'm so sorry. I'm so sorry for whatever I did. Or didn't do.

ELEANOR   You'll write it down. Everything about the attempted land amalgamation and Elizabeth's part in it.

PARRY   I'll write it all down. All I know.

> *ELEANOR throws PARRY a dry towel.*

ELEANOR   Now clean yourself up. Pathetic little faggot.

> *PARRY dries himself. TED enters with BESS.*

TED   Oh. Dear. It looks like Eleanor's just finishing up in here. I'll . . . well. I'll go get some . . . refreshments, or. Coffee, Eleanor?

ELEANOR   Thanks.

TED   Come on then, Parry. Let's get you some dry clothes.

> *PARRY and BESS exchange looks.*

PARRY   Unauthorized accounting procedures: I-I told her.

> *TED takes PARRY by the arm and leads him out.*

           (to TED) It's my fault.

BESS   *(to TED, as he goes)* I'll have tea, please.

TED   *(as he goes)* I'll see what I can dig up!

> ELEANOR *takes up her seat at the table.* BESS *stays standing, looking after* PARRY.

BESS What did you do to Parry.

ELEANOR What I can't do to you.

If you would corrobo / rate

BESS How can I corroborate if I don't know what he said?

ELEANOR You know. I know you know.

BESS *(her anger slipping slightly)* What if I don't know? What if there's no proof? When will you be satisfied?

> ELEANOR *and* BESS *sit in stalemate for a moment. Then* ELEANOR *takes out a package of letters.*

(the letters) Those are mine.

ELEANOR That's one question out of the way.

BESS How did you get my letters?

> ELEANOR *places the letters in between her and* BESS. BESS *considers the letters with rising anxiety.*

How did you—?

ELEANOR We'll . . . wait for Ted, shall we?

> *In time* TED *returns with a coffee for* ELEANOR.

TED No tea. Sorry.

(to ELEANOR*)* Parry had a slight seizure.

BESS / He—?

TED He's resting.

(to ELEANOR*)* Should be fine to see you again tomorrow.

BESS Stop. No more of this. I'll tell you what you want to know.

> BESS *wriggles in her chair, keeping one eye on the letters.*

Parry did meet with Thom. They discussed the patents on my land. Ashley met with him, too. They spoke of possible . . . well . . . dating. But I didn't seriously consider it.

ELEANOR You "didn't seriously" . . . ?

BESS They—well, I rely on them—Ashley and Parry—and they never make errors in judgment. They're completely competent. They should never have been brought here. It's not their fault.

ELEANOR *(to TED, exasperated)* They're singing three parts to the same song.

(to BESS) And they've all agreed on the key!

BESS I don't mean to—

TED *(frustrated, but nonetheless paternal)* Here's the thing, Bess: I follow lines of inquiry in this case and in one way or another they keep leading back to you. I can't ignore that. I'm not *allowed* to ignore that. If I turn a blind eye to all the arrows that point in your direction . . . then I'm no longer fit to do my job. Where does that leave Eddie? Mary? Thom? If you don't learn to take responsibility for the decisions you make, where does that leave you? No. We have no choice. We continue to persuade your friends to speak, or . . .

TED leans across the table and picks up the packet of letters.

we get the public involved.

BESS The public? Involved how?

ELEANOR People are inordinately fascinated by the private correspondence of celebrities.

BESS is a little cocky.

BESS There is nothing in any letter of mine to incriminate me in this case.

ELEANOR People draw conclusions according to their own bias. We're now ready to manipulate that bias, that's all.

TED hands ELEANOR two of the letters.

A letter, an account, a scrap of conversation . . . take them separately? They mean nothing. But accumulate them? They show trends, expose propensities. We pile these things together.

ELEANOR places a letter:

A note here from Ashley, *(another letter)* and one from Parry, confirming the admiral's intent to marry you.

Another letter.

Your reply, stating your consideration of said marriage.

BESS The contents of that letter are completely ambiguous.

ELEANOR Indeed they are. Intentionally vague. Suggesting collusion.

Another letter.

From Thom, now, regarding your physical intimacy:

BESS recognizes the letter.

BESS *(horrified)* Stop talking.

ELEANOR *(reading)* "I long for word from your own hand, and cannot help but inquire whether your great buttocks are grown any less / or no?"

BESS How did you / get that?

ELEANOR Singing a little descant / now?

TED grabs the letter.

TED *(reading)* "I cannot help but inquire whether *your great buttocks* are grown any less or no?"

TED holds up the letter.

You heard it here / first!

BESS	You don't know the backstory.
ELEANOR	*(amused)* The backstory.
BESS	*(gaining fury)* All those letters *prove* is that Thom made jokes about my, my . . . *behind.* That we shared grief over the death of his wife and my mother. That there was talk of our relationship taking another form, *which it never did.*
ELEANOR	If you think public opinion relies on fact, think again. *(holding up* THOM's *letter)* They're gonna love this.
BESS	The size of my *bum* has nothing to do with treason!!

> BESS *gets up from the table.*

Those letters are private. You're disgusting.

> BESS *barely contains her tears of rage.*

Am I free to go?

> TED *looks at* ELEANOR.

TED	Gee, I guess that's it, Eleanor. The princess is finished with us.

> He starts to gather the dishes and paperwork.

Time to pack up and go.

> BESS *starts for the door.*

Oh, on your way home, please consider how sorry I am about the leak this morning.

BESS	Pardon?
TED	Don't lose sleep over it. How many people do you know that read the tabloids.
BESS	What leak?
TED	That you've been arrested. Imprisoned in the Tower. Oh. That you're pregnant by the Lord High / Admiral.

BESS	You told / the *papers*?!
TED	That you went along with Thom's whole plot. That you're not smart enough to see the implications of your actions.
ELEANOR	Just an average teenager overwhelmed by romantic notions.
BESS	I was never— Average?
TED	The truth is immaterial once the public have their story.
BESS	You can't do this!

TED takes off his jolly uncle mask.

TED	I can do *WHATEVER I PLEASE*! You! Don't seem to be taking into consideration the seriousness of these interviews! The peril that might ensue!

BESS takes on TED.

BESS	The tabloids can't publish unsubstantiated rumours.
TED	The tabloids publish whatever I tell them to publish.
BESS	That's not fair.
TED	*(amused)* From the mouths of babes.
BESS	I'll expose you. You'll be punished.
TED	By who? Eleanor? Eddie?
BESS	The people love ME!
TED	Who cares what "the people" think!

BESS starts to pace and panic.

BESS	*(a new tack)* I'll tell them that you're not a cognate! / That
TED	Yes.
BESS	my father never wanted you in charge, / that
TED	Yes.

BESS	you bribed the Council to kick Kate out and make *you* / Protector—
TED	Yes. Please! Tell them again and again.
BESS	That you and Eleanor—

> *BESS stops mid-thought and looks at TED.*

No. Why?

Why would you *want* me to tell them that?

TED	*(coyly)* My lips are sealed.

> *BESS circles in frustration. The dawn breaks: if she shoots her mouth off she can be dismissed as a rebellious, entitled teenager. TED and ELEANOR are counting on that so they can discredit her publicly.*

BESS	No way will I expose you. I won't go on the offensive when I am so obviously outmanned and outgunned.

You underestimate me and what I'm capable of.

I have never lied.

TED	Is that so.

> *BESS creates a flank and shoots broadside.*

BESS	I am the victim of a slanderous assault.
TED	A victim?!
BESS	*(cleanly)* It's not my responsibility to clear my own name. If I . . . come out swinging, it'll look like I'm *guilty*, like I have something to *hide*, to *defend*.
TED	Treason is a serious charge.
BESS	I won't be judged for my *ethics* as well as my morals. No way. I won't throw you under the boat in order to save myself. I'll thrive on my own merit, thank you very much.

TED	You're fifteen! What kind of "merit" can you possibly have earned?
BESS	Innocence. The people know me. They see me for who I am.
TED	I will sink you, little Bess. This is not the end.
BESS	Then you'll have to prove I'm lying. *That* is your burden. Now. If you'll excuse me, I'm going to find a cup of tea. That is, if I'm free to go?
TED	Yeah. Get the hell out of my sight!

BESS goes. TED and ELEANOR stew for a moment.

ELEANOR	Thom. Thom has to talk now. You have to get Thom to talk.

ELEANOR stands. TED bashes one of the tumblers off the table.

GIRL POWER—MARCH 3, 1549

In public. At night. It's raining. A woman with her hood up walks quickly by. A few moments later BESS appears with an umbrella up. She finds shelter and puts the umbrella down, shaking off the water. She looks around. She waits. The woman in the hood returns, looks around, joins her under the shelter.

MARY	I thought I made myself perfectly clear about the weather and my coming out in it.
BESS	I'll get you some new boots.
MARY	You can get me a new doctor. I've worn out the last one.

MARY looks at BESS, who looks at MARY.

Is this thing not over yet with you?

BESS	It's getting worse.
MARY	How can it possibly?

BESS instructs MARY by putting her hands on her belly.

(dawning) Awh crap. You're kidding me.

BESS	It's not my / fault!
MARY	Luck is not exactly your strong suit right now, / is it.
BESS	Doooon't! I have enough people yelling at / me!
MARY	Sir Thomas Muttonhead strikes again.
BESS	I need to take care of it. There are ways to take care of it, right? People to see.
MARY	I'm sure there are, but you're not going to see one.
BESS	I have to.
MARY	You're the daughter of a king. The sister of a king.
BESS	Exactly.
MARY	You can't. Do that?
BESS	I can't do this. A bastard, Mary.
MARY	Yes.
BESS	Like you. / Like me.
MARY	*(correcting her)* I am not—

We are managing just fine.

BESS	*(slightly petulant)* I won't be responsible for that. Not when I did nothing wrong.
MARY	*(incredulously)* You. Did nothing wrong.
BESS	Not in that department.
MARY	So, now, what? I'm supposed to take care of this, too? I cannot believe you want me to—

BESS	I need your help. Really. *Really.*
MARY	Good Lord. Is this what parenting feels like?

A moment.

Have you seen Thom?

BESS	No.
MARY & BESS	I—
MARY	Speak.
BESS	I wish I could see him. Is that weird?
MARY	Super weird.
BESS	I wonder how he is.
MARY	He broke your heart!
BESS	I have a feeling / that—
MARY	And then he broke your hymen!
BESS	Maryyy!

A moment.

Is this what justice feels like?

MARY	Being pregnant?
BESS	Cut it out.
MARY	Someone will.
BESS	Thom's gonna die—if he doesn't tell on me—probably even if he does. I've killed him.
MARY	Well . . .
BESS	Haven't I?
MARY	Yup.

BESS	A fifteen-year-old girl can do that.
MARY	Apparently.
BESS	Wild.

A moment.

What do I do next? What else am I capable of?

MARY	Abortion.
BESS	Don't say—! That sounds so—
MARY	If you're going to do it, you're going to call it what it is.

BESS and MARY stand together, looking out at the rain.

BESS	Abortion.
MARY	Are you sad even? A little?
BESS	That's the feeling I have. Like I can't feel anything.

Except I wanna barf.

A moment.

Mary . . . ?

MARY	What.
BESS	If I . . . dreamed about it, does that mean I wanted it?
MARY	Absolutely not. Absolutely. Not.

A moment.

BESS	Where do I go?
MARY	You think I know? I am officially opposed to any—

BESS looks at MARY, who looks at BESS.

(sighing) Oh . . . bother. I'll do some research. Is there anything you do that *doesn't* get you into trouble?

BESS	Will I get out of this?

MARY   If Thom keeps his mouth shut.

BESS   I have to clean him out. Like he never existed.

MARY   If only.

BESS   To recreate my virginity.

MARY   Really.

BESS   I can be a virgin. I can be anything I set my mind to.

MARY   Believe that.

BESS   I do.

MARY   Me too.

BESS   Then you'll help me?

MARY   You drive me nuts.

MARY puts up her umbrella.

When I find out where, I'll let you know. *(harshly)* Sooner than later. And don't get into any more trouble, okay?

BESS   Okay.

MARY stifles a sneeze.

MARY   Great.

MARY goes. BESS walks out of the shelter. She lifts her face, and is cleansed by the rain.

INTERVIEW SIX: TEA AND TRUMP—
MARCH 5, 1549

At table. ELEANOR *sits at one end of the table. At the vacant end is a full silver tea service.* TED *enters with* PARRY *and* ASHLEY. PARRY *is still shaking.* ASHLEY's *arms hang limply at her sides.*

TED   Won't this be nice? The princess is coming to tea!

TED pulls out the empty chair across from ELEANOR. *He gestures toward* ASHLEY.

I bet you could use a little rest for those weary limbs.

ASHLEY *refuses to sit.*

ASHLEY   Don't you worry about me.

TED   No need to get tetchy. I'm only . . . acting the gentleman.

So shiny! Look at the silver, Eleanor. Aren't you excited?

ELEANOR   Not really.

TED looks at ELEANOR, *then back at the others.*

TED   Prefers a good cup o' joe, does our Eleanor.

After a moment BESS *enters, no longer dressed like a girl.*

Bess! How handsome!

TED notices that BESS *is paralyzed at the sight of her friends.*

Of course. You weren't expecting your friends.

Look! Tea! A whole pot. To start our final day.

BESS   Is it over?

TED   I can't believe it took us this long to find tea. In England.

(to ELEANOR*)* I'd say an eye test is in order for you, my dear.

(to BESS) Why don't you be mother and pour.

BESS   I don't want to pour.

TED   It's your party.

BESS   I'm not playing along—

TED   It's not a game.

Pour.

Please.

> *BESS pours a cup of tea for PARRY, who warms his hands on the cup, and for ASHLEY, who stares at the cup longingly but is unable to raise her hands to lift it. As she pours:*

I wanted you to know your pals are doing fine. Oh, oh, oh: and I brought their signed statements.

> *TED places documents on top of BESS's tea cup.*

Go ahead. You'll find summaries on page two.

> *BESS is ashamed and half breathless. She peruses the documents for some time and with great care, under the gaze of the others.*

Ashley was a rock. Parry . . . a bit of a softy: let a few things slip.

ASHLEY   *(like a match to paper)* You lying little worm!!

PARRY   I / didn't

ASHLEY   You promised / you would never—

PARRY   / I couldn't help it!

BESS   Ashley—

ASHLEY   Dragged behind horses / till dead!

PARRY   I was / drowning!

BESS   *(to ASHLEY)* Ted's playing / you!

ASHLEY	He promised—
BESS	It was no small matter for him to make that promise. And a bigger one to break it. *If* he did.
PARRY	Oh, Messy-one . . .
BESS	You all right?

BESS watches while PARRY weeps silently. She watches ASHLEY hang her head. Then she gathers her wits to present her closing remarks.

May I say—Ted, Eleanor—I feel deeply chastened reading the details of my private family life, written out as they are here in cold, inadequate terms, and elicited under unrelenting compulsion. I see why you think I'm no equal to you: I look silly, childish even, not worthy of the stature of my birth. And it's certain that neither Ashley nor Parry conducted themselves in a manner befitting their positions in my household.

Still. No one who reads these documents can possibly understand that we are a *family*, bound not by blood, but by love.

ELEANOR	Love?
BESS	The information you have coerced from my friends, and indeed from me, is unseemly, perhaps even shameful, but in no way does it constitute proof of treason. You have no hard evidence of my complicity in any plot.

BESS swallows, then plays her card.

You have no witness who will speak against me, no one to tie me to any of the charges brought against the admiral. Have you.

A moment.

TED	Have we. Eleanor?

ELEANOR	Why don't you check?
TED	I'll just poke my nose out the door here and see.

TED goes. BESS looks at ASHLEY and PARRY, who both look back at her. ELEANOR betrays the smallest trace of pleasure as she watches BESS squirm.

BESS	Where is he going?
ELEANOR	Where do you think?

TED returns with THOM. THOM is changed. There is an abandon in him. An unpredictability. BESS sees this.

TED   Look what I found wandering the halls. A witness!

A moment while TED and ELEANOR allow BESS to stare at THOM. He meets her gaze, unfazed.

(to THOM) Right, now, Thommie.

This *girl* believes with all her heart that you're a chump and a patsy. She set you up, and she'll *walk*. Take all that happened between you and sweep it under the carpet. Speak, brother. Show her! This is your last chance.

BESS holds her breath.

THOM	I'll speak for the whole world to hear. At my trial.
TED	No, no, no, you need to talk *now*. The Council's heading to Parliament with an act of attainder. There is no trial.

This lands on both THOM and BESS.

BESS	No trial?
THOM	Sheets and water, but no due process.
TED	You shot the dog.
THOM	He was growling at me.
ELEANOR	*(to BESS)* No trial.

TED You were in the king's chamber with a gun! You've gotta tell us how you got to that point—

THOM No. I'll speak on the stand, on public record. I'll tell all of England what they need to hear.

TED England won't hear you, not until you're standing at the block! *(of BESS)* Accuse her! Implicate her! Please! The case will explode. We'll show them who was really at the helm.

THOM Not the admiral.

TED It was *her.* Say so.

THOM *(seeing TED's ploy)* To save my own neck.

TED Yes.

ELEANOR grips her jaw.

THOM No. There was a time I thought, that to *live*, to *live* . . . well, you do anything in your power just to live. Compromise. Anything.

THOM looks at BESS. She reveals nothing.

At what cost, brother.

ELEANOR shakes her head at BESS.

Thank you very much for your fraternal concern. I'll take what's coming to me.

She . . . is innocent. So innocent. Ha! I've seen the light.

TED You've what?

THOM *(singing)** *And what should that rare mirror be,*
Some goddess or some queen is she . . .

ELEANOR No use.

THOM gets to his knees in front of BESS.

---

* "Say Love If Ever Thou Didst Find" by John Dowland.

THOM	Forgive me: I have a soul to save as much as other folks.
	(a summation) And with the mercy of the virgin I will enter paradise.

TED pulls THOM to his feet, away from BESS.

TED	Get away from— Don't kneel— *I* have to sign the order for your execution!
ELEANOR	There's no point / in trying—
TED	*(to THOM)* My name! Next to yours!
THOM	*(triumphantly)* "Now art thou cursed. A fugitive and a vagabond shalt thou be / on the earth."**
ELEANOR	He won't / turn—
TED	I just now had to stand up in front of Parliament and declare that my allegiance to the king was more important than the life of my brother!
THOM	Ha! How did that go?
TED	*(to ELEANOR)* Don't make me kill him. I can't kill him.
ELEANOR	Take a seat.

TED collapses in one of the chairs.

THOM	You're afraid. Aren't you Ted.
TED	Yes. I'm afraid.
THOM	The writing's on the wall.
ELEANOR	Was the princess behind this? Did she devise the plot?
THOM	*(gleefully)* No one will ever know.
ELEANOR	*(shaking her head)* You always fell for the girls, didn't you. You never were smart enough / to see a

---

** Genesis 4:11–12, King James Version.

Like lightning BESS *flies at* ELEANOR *and hits at her:*

BESS He is smarter than you will ever be! I will / not have him insulted—

ELEANOR He's a fool and / so is his brother—

BESS Do you hear me!

ELEANOR / I hear you. We all hear you.

BESS I will not!

> BESS *looks at* THOM *one last time, pulls herself together to make an exit befitting a princess.*

I believe we have answered your questions to the degree that our memory will attest.

(to ELEANOR*)* We recognize your office in maintaining the security of our nation and we apologize for taking up so much of the taxpayers' time and resources.

> BESS *goes to leave. She stops. She turns and looks at* THOM.

See you, Thom.

THOM See you, Bess.

> *A moment.*

BESS *(to* ASHLEY *and* PARRY*)* Let's go home.

ELEANOR Oh, they're not going with you.

BESS *(defiantly)* They sure are.

> *As* ASHLEY *and* PARRY *begin to follow* BESS:

ELEANOR Stop. Right. There.

> ASHLEY *and* PARRY *stop.* BESS *doesn't flinch.* ELEANOR *takes her time.*

(to BESS*)* I'm surprised, and a little delighted, that you "*recognize my office.*" Well, I recognize your office, too. You're

an artist, aren't you. At least that's how you fancy yourself. You select facts, opinions, memories to create a portrait that you want people to see. That you constantly keep on show. You surround yourself with sycophants of half your mental capacity because they buy into that picture.

I don't.

Your lies, your manipulation, your arrogance: that's the real you. That's the portrait I want the world to see. Not such a pretty picture.

BESS   Can I *please* take my friends home?

ELEANOR   I'm afraid not. Ashley and Parry are staying here a while / longer . . .

ASHLEY   / No!

PARRY   / Oh God.

ASHLEY sits with no expression. PARRY now weeps audibly.

BESS   Why?

ELEANOR   The Council has deemed them inappropriate companions for the king's sister. You need discipline. We'll do a search for suitable replacements, but for the time being . . . I will be acting as your governess.

BESS   *(to ELEANOR)* You Will NOT!

(to TED) SHE / WILL NOT!

As ELEANOR escorts BESS, who is in full tirade, from the room:

ELEANOR   Let's / get you home for lunch.

BESS   *(to ELEANOR)* Ashley is my governess!

(to TED) I will not stand this, Ted! I'm gonna tell everyone what you did to me in here! I'll tell Eddie! You'll—

(to ELEANOR) Get your hands off me, you bitch—

(to TED) You'll, you'll be sorry you ever fucked with / me!

ELEANOR You spoiled / little tramp.

BESS You stupid, ugly cow!

> *The shouts of the exiting women echo through the room.*
> *THOM holds out his bound hands to TED. TED turns away*
> *from THOM. He takes ASHLEY and PARRY each by the arm*
> *and leads them out.*

MYTH-MAKING—MARCH 20, 1549

> *In public. THOM stands alone, awaiting his execution. He*
> *is in a state of revelation and euphoria.*

THOM She is Astraea: come down to earth from the celestial realm!
She will restore her people to an age of glory! She holds
the scales of justice in her hand and the scorpion lies dead
under her feet! Follow her! Follow her, or England will
meet its doom!

> *At bed. BESS is sleeping, dreaming fitfully. MARY sits beside*
> *her. BESS begins to awaken.*

BESS Follow . . .

MARY Finally! Here you / come.

BESS Follow . . . / follow—

MARY Up through the purple / haze.

BESS . . . or England will— Oh.

I'm here, not. Doom.

Thom is . . . ?

MARY   It's all finished.

BESS   Is it?

MARY   You gonna barf? You need a bucket?

BESS   / Is he—

MARY   Man, everything smells in here.

The nurse said it'll last a day or two: the cramping. Three at most. The bleeding might be as long as a week. They'll give you some pills to help.

I cannot believe I am sitting with you in a place like this.

BESS   I want to cry. I'm going to cry.

MARY   I'm not stopping you. Feel what you feel.

BESS   I feel sick.

MARY picks up a wastebasket.

MARY   Here's the bucket.

BESS leans over it and closes her eyes.

THOM reappears.

THOM   *(singing his anthem at the top of his lungs)**** *To her then yield thy shafts and bow,*
That can command affections so:
Love is free,
So are her thoughts that vanquish thee
There is no queen of love but she,
She, she, she, she, and only she,
Only queen of love and—

THOM disappears. BESS grabs MARY's arm as she opens her eyes.

MARY   / Ow.

***   "Say Love If Ever Thou Didst Find" by John Dowland.

BESS	Is he dead? Did he die?
MARY	He didn't go quietly.
BESS	Don't—don't tell me that!
MARY	Mea / culpa.
BESS	Why would you tell me / that?!
MARY	Don't yell at me! He cursed a lot. The rest was quick.
BESS	*(not wanting to hear)* Aaaaaahhh!!
MARY	Two strokes.
	Finito.
BESS	Ted finally signed the order?
MARY	He couldn't. No point forcing him.
	Eddie signed it. The Council clapped and cheered. I guess signing someone's death warrant gets you in their club.
	We'll see how long Ted lasts now.
BESS	Why?
MARY	You can't kill your sibling. No one will trust you again.
	MARY looks around at their undistinguished surroundings. She considers her past and her future. She looks at BESS.
	Should one ever have a baby.
BESS	No.
MARY	Makes ya think. Don' it?
	A moment.
BESS	My head hurts.
MARY	Good. At least you feel something. You'll go home now. Start to repair the rotten mess you've made.
BESS	It's gone.

MARY   What.

BESS   The rotten mess. Gone. The danger.

No more explosions, no more storms. I'm pure now.

Pure . . . luminous . . . light. I will look for the Winter Circle and see my perfect virginity.

MARY   We'll get you some more of those nice yellow pills on the way out. Can you walk?

MARY helps BESS up. BESS stops her for a moment, just before they go.

BESS   This day died a man with much wit and very little judgment.

MARY   I wish there were no more in England.

MARY starts off. BESS stops.

BESS   I'm a Virgo.

MARY   Since the day you were born.

BESS   Virgo intacta.

MARY   Come on, little girl.

MARY goes. BESS is bathed in white light and there are strains of heavenly music.

End of Act Two.

SCENE BREAKDOWN IN CHRONOLOGICAL ORDER

(many of these dates are approximate)

An Apt Vessel—February 1547
Say Yes to the Dress—June 1547
Hide and Seek—August 1547
Unaccompanied Minor—January 4, 1548
Impropriety—June 1548
Exile—June 1548
Commander—November 1548
Crash—January 14, 1549
Burn—January 16, 1549
Whitewashing—January 17, 1549
Interview One—January 19, 1549
Interview Two—January 19, 1549
Interview Three, Part One—January 19, 1549
Intervention—January 19, 1549
Interview Three, Part Two—January 19, 1549
Hidden Motive One—January 20, 1549
Hidden Motive Two—January 20, 1549
Shreds—January 20, 1549
Interview Four—January 21, 1549
Ashley's Torture—January 21, 1549
Silhouette—February 21, 1549
Off the Record—February 21, 1549
Parry's Torture / Interview Five—February 28, 1549
Girl Power—March 3, 1549
Interview Six—Tea and Trump—March 5, 1549
Myth-Making—March 20, 1549

ACKNOWLEDGEMENTS

Stratford Festival. Banff Playwrights Colony. Ontario Arts Council. Canada Council for the Arts. Newton Awards (Shaw Festival). Andy McKim. Bob White. Monica Dufault and Essential Collective Theatre. John Stead.

Actors who worked on the development of this play: Tess Benger, Gray Powell, Patrick McManus, Kelli Fox, Julia Course, Fiona Byrne, Billy Lake, Bahia Watson, Gareth Potter, Kevin Bundy, Yanna McIntosh, Sara Farb, Shannon Taylor, André Morin, Christopher Morris, Stephen Ouimette, Claire Lautier, Maev Beaty, Ruby Joy, Ron Kennell, Brad Hodder, Nigel Bennett, Jenny Young, and Jessica Severin (stage manager).

Kate Hennig is a diverse, multi-award-winning theatre artist: a playwright, performer, teacher, and Associate Artistic Director of the Shaw Festival. Kate's first play, *The Last Wife*, which premiered at the Stratford Festival in 2015, was met with rave reviews and has had five further productions with another four productions scheduled. Kate is currently writing *Father's Daughter*, the third play in the Tudor queens series. Born in England and raised in Alberta, she lives and writes in Stratford, Ontario. Visit www.katehennig.com for more information.

First edition: June 2017
Printed and bound in Canada by Imprimerie Gauvin, Gatineau

Cover photo by Korhan Kalabak
Author photo © David Cooper

**PLAYWRIGHTS
CANADA PRESS**

202-269 Richmond St. W.
Toronto, ON
M5V 1X1

416.703.0013
info@playwrightscanada.com
www.playwrightscanada.com
@playcanpress

FSC
www.fsc.org

MIX
Paper from
responsible sources
FSC® C100212